I0161269

THE HEALING MODEL

By
Bill Chambers

TEACH Services, Inc.
Brushton, New York

**PRINTED IN
THE UNITED STATES OF AMERICA**

World rights reserved. This book or any portion thereof may not be copied or reproduced in any form or manner whatever, except as provided by law, without the written permission of the publisher, except by a reviewer who may quote brief passages in a review. The author assumes full responsibility for the accuracy of all facts and quotations as cited in this book.

2009 10 11 12 13 14 · 5 4 3 2 1

Copyright © 2009 Bill Chambers and TEACH Services, Inc.
ISBN-13: 978-1-57258-581-2
ISBN-10: 1-57258-581-1
Library of Congress Control Number: 2009933834

Published by

TEACH Services, Inc.
www.TEACHServices.com

CONTENTS

INTRODUCTION

"Before destruction the heart of man is haughty, and before honour is humility. He that answereth a matter before he heareth it, it is folly and shame unto him" *(Proverbs 18:12, 13).*

This is not a book written to entertain or leave the reader with warm fuzzy feelings. This is a book written for study. It is written with the hope that the reader will approach the message contained within with a humble spirit and an open mind. I have learned the folly of being close-minded.

God only knows how many good people have forfeited wonderful knowledge and comfort to their souls because they would not read or listen to someone that was not of their persuasion or church denomination or maybe because they had heard some negative report about that person from someone else. Even if you do not initially agree with what you read in these pages, I hope you will be provoked to search the Scriptures to test whether these things are true.

At the time of the completing of this book, I am sixty-five years old. I have had many good and many bad experiences in life, but none of which has been more rewarding and fulfilling than the study of God's Word and learning more about His gracious ways and His great desire to save His wayward children.

I am not a theologian, Bible scholar, or seminary professor. I do not hold a doctorate or have a lot of formal education. However, I have spent untold hours reading, studying, and meditating upon the writings of the Holy Scriptures as well as the works of those who are qualified to call themselves theologians, Bible scholars, doctors, and professors.

In my study and through personal experience, I have found that God meets us where we are and leads us no faster than we are able to follow. I believe that the Christian believer should never become stagnant but should be continually seeking, learning, and "growing in the grace and knowledge of Jesus Christ" (2 Peter 3:18). But each person must be allowed to grow at his or her own pace.

The message contained in this book is one that even I may not have accepted ten years ago. I'm not sure I was spiritually ready for it. At that time, I was closed-minded to certain issues. Therefore, I realize that some who read this book may not be ready for its message either. Having said that, I also want to point out that the message of salvation in this book is not intended to deny any other acceptable way of understanding salvation, but it is intended to show what I believe is a more progressive model of God's wonderful plan to save and restore His children. And more than that, hopefully you will see God in a whole new way that will bring a real peace and joy to your heart and life.

I have attempted to put into my own words a way of understanding the issues involved in salvation that are logical and clear. I have made an attempt to write this book in such a way that any person who can read should be able to comprehend its message. It is in this spirit that I present this work for your consideration.

Chapter One

DARK SPEECH

"My servant Moses is not so, who is faithful in all mine house. With him will I speak mouth to mouth, even apparently, and not in dark speeches; and the similitude of the LORD shall he behold" (Numbers 12:7, 8).

Once, an old farmer was attending a board meeting in the little country church where he had been a member most of his life. During the meeting, the pastor brought up the suggestion that the church purchase a chandelier for the sanctuary. The old farmer was quick to respond. He stood up and said, "Preacher, I know you mean well, but I'm agin it; first of all, we ain't got nobody who knows how to play one of them thangs, and besides that, what we really need is some more lights in here!"

This story is told as a joke, but one of the things that make it so laughable is that we all know it really could have happened. Too many people in our "enlightened age," because of innocent ignorance, are left in the dark. The reason for much of this is the misunderstanding of words and terms used by others who may not even know the meaning themselves.

There is a lot of this kind of "dark speech" in the Christian church today. By the term dark speech, I mean words and expressions in which the definitions are not known or are difficult to comprehend or understand. Unfortunately, the Christian "clichés" and "theological" words and terms that we sometimes hear, we often repeat when we don't really know what they mean.

This dark speech is heard in sermons and Sabbath classes, sung in the songs of church hymnals, and read in our Christian literature. It has become commonplace, and the average Christian has become so accustomed to it that most are unaware of its existence. You, dear reader, may be unaware of it. I hope this will not be the case after you have read this chapter.

Jesus, speaking to the Jews who were seeking to kill Him because He claimed that He was the Son of God, said, "[you] search the scriptures; for in them ye think ye have eternal life: and they are they which testify of me. And ye will not come to me, that ye might have life" (John 5:39-40).

Jesus was implying that it is possible for a person to search and study the Scriptures and still not know God. If we aren't studying the Bible to know God better, chances are we may be doing it for the wrong reason! But the point I want to make in this chapter is this: we could find ourselves in the same place spiritually as the Jews Jesus was speaking to long ago if we let dark speech—misinterpretation, poor translation, or misunderstanding—affect our study of the Bible. Instead of revealing the truth about God, dark speech may rather contribute to the development of the wrong understanding of Him.

Christians in this age, an age that may culminate with the second coming of Christ, especially need to know God, not only intellectually and spiritually, but also personally and intimately, like a close friend. The Bible, when using the word "know" in this way, implies more than simply being introduced or knowing "about" someone; it implies a close, intimate relationship. A relationship like that of close friends or a husband and wife who truly love and honor one another, like God had with Moses and Abraham, who were called the "friends of God."

Communication is critical to relationships, especially intimate ones. Exodus 33:11 tells us, "And the LORD spake unto Moses face to face, as a man speaketh unto his friend." We can learn how God speaks to His friends by examining how God spoke to Moses.

Numbers 12:8 says, "With him [Moses] will I speak mouth to mouth, even apparently, and not in dark speeches; and the similitude of the LORD shall he behold."

First, this verse says God spoke to Moses "mouth to mouth," that is, with no one in between Him and Moses. This was demonstrated when God called Moses up on Mt. Sinai to receive the Ten Commandments:

> "And all the people saw the thunderings, and the lightnings, and the noise of the trumpet, and the mountain smoking: and when the people saw it, they removed, and stood afar off. And they said unto Moses, Speak thou with us, and we will hear: but let not God speak with us, lest we die. And Moses said unto the people, Fear not: for God is come to prove you, and that his fear may be before your faces, that ye sin not. And the people stood afar off, and Moses drew near unto the thick darkness where God was" (Exodus 20:18-21).

The people "stood afar off" because they were afraid of God, but Moses, because of his personal relationship with God, knew that there was no reason to be afraid. Some Christians have been taught that we must have a "go between," meaning a special holy person between us and God. Yet in reality, if we have a relationship with God, we need no one between us and Him. Notice that there was no one between God and Moses when he went up on the mountain!

Once we learn the truth about God, we will know there is absolutely no reason to be afraid of our heavenly Father. Jesus, in coming to this world, revealed that God himself, in the person of Christ, came to be our intercessor or intermediary. We could not go to heaven to find God, so He came down to find us! How good of Him to do that.

Let's turn back to Numbers 12. Now that we understand the term mouth to mouth, what does "even apparently" mean? It is from a Hebrew word meaning "clearly," and it is immediately followed by the phrase "not in dark speeches." This passage tells us that God prefers to speak to His friends, like Moses, clearly, not in puzzles or riddles, or symbolic, figurative language. Furthermore, there is no need for someone to act as a go between. God wants this kind of relationship with His people yet today, and as we noted earlier, Jesus came to help us with that.

The Lord said that He considers His followers His friends and He does not want them in the dark, misunderstanding and ignorant of the truth. He said, "Henceforth I call you not servants; for the servant knoweth not what his lord doeth: but I have called you friends; for all things that I have heard of my Father I have made known unto you" (John 15:15).

Did you catch that last part? "I have called you friends; for all things that I have heard of my Father I have made known unto you."

The problem was, and still is today, that a lot of what Jesus said to the disciples they did not comprehend because of the traditional beliefs they had been taught all their lives. Many things Jesus said seemed like strange talk to them; that is why Jesus said what He did in the following passage:

> "These things have I spoken unto you in proverbs [or figures of speech]: but the time cometh, when I shall no more speak unto you in proverbs, but I shall shew you plainly of the Father. At that day ye shall ask in my name: and I say not unto you, that I will pray the Father for you: For the Father himself loveth you, because ye have loved me, and have believed that I came out from God. I came forth from the Father, and am come into the world: again, I leave the world, and go to the Father. His disciples said unto him, Lo, now speakest thou plainly, and speakest no proverb" (John 16:25-29).

Here, even though He spoke to the disciples plainly, they still didn't understand everything Jesus wanted them to know. But the day would come when they would no longer need types and figures, parables, or symbols. The day would come when they would understand the truth about God the Father and the things Jesus had told them would become clear, and at that moment, it would no longer sound like dark speech. That day finally came for them after Christ's resurrection and the outpouring of the Holy Spirit.

But what about us? Do we hear a lot of dark speech today in the church? What about the Christian clichés we hear? Terms such as "covered by the blood", "praying in the spirit", or "righteousness by faith". These are precious phrases that have been used by many Christians. We sing them from the hymnal and hear them from the pulpit, but many of these terms can't be found in the Bible. I would dare-say that very few of us have a good understanding of what many of these phrases really mean.

Then there are words such as propitiation, justification, and sanctification. These words are in the Bible, and we hear them read often; yet few of us know their true meaning. Many books have been written on justification and sanctification, often only to make them seem more complicated than before. They seem like just more dark speech.

Adding to this problem, over the years, many of the words used in the widely accepted King James Version Bible have become antiquated or outdated. For example, the word "wist," commonly used in England in 1611, has long since been replaced with the word "know." Some words mean exactly the opposite of what they did when the KJV translation was first completed. For example, the term "by and by" in the KJV was translated from the Greek word "eutheos," which means "immediately" or "at once." That was the meaning of the term by and by in England in 1611. But today, by and by means just the opposite. Today it means not immediately, but sometime later.

Another example is the word "atonement." The origin of this word dates back to the 1400s when it originally meant, "to unite," "to reconcile," literally, "to be at one," thus at-one-ment or atonement. But in the 1600s, the word came to be understood as "appeasement," which is the same as the Latin word "propitiation," which we find in most Bibles. Today, in modern dictionaries the original definition of atonement, which was "reconciliation," is listed as obsolete, and in its place is listed the definition "to atone for" or "to appease."

An example of the use of the word atonement as we understand it today would be something like this: If I forget my wife's birthday, then I must do something special, like bring her a dozen roses, to make "atonement" or to "atone" for my shortcoming in forgetting her birthday. I must "appease" her so she will not be angry anymore and forgive me.

Because of this change in the meaning of the word atonement, many believe Christ's death on the cross was to "atone" or "appease" God's anger so we can be forgiven and brought back into His good graces again. This can have serious spiritual implications. Many Christians see the atonement of Christ in a way that reflects poorly on the character of God. We will discuss this in detail in another chapter.

Since the Scriptures were originally written in Hebrew and Greek, we can see how the use of words that accurately reflects the original words is critical for the reader to better understand what the prophets intended to say. Some modern translations have done this to some extent. For example, some now use "set right" in place of justification, "keep right" instead of sanctification, and "reconciliation" or "atonement" instead of propitiation. These more correctly reflect the meaning of the original words and are certainly easier for us to understand.

Unfortunately, I believe many people think that if they are a good Christian they should know these terms and their meanings and are therefore ashamed to ask, "What does that mean?" But remember, Jesus said that to enter into the kingdom we must "become as little children," that is, being humble, teachable, and anxious to learn. So don't be afraid to ask questions!

A gifted speaker once wrote: "A little girl once asked me, "Are you going to speak this afternoon?" "No, not this afternoon," I replied. "I am very sorry," she said. "I thought you were going to speak, and I asked several of my friends to come. Will you please ask the minister to speak easy words *that we can understand? Will you please tell him that we do not understand large words, like 'justification' and 'sanctification'? We do not know what these words mean."* (*Counsels to Parents, Teachers, and Students*, p. 254).

The little girl's complaint contains a lesson worthy of consideration. There are many who would do well to heed the request, *"speak easy words that we may know what you mean."* Teachers and preachers should follow the example of Jesus who taught so simply that all, even the children, could understand.

Amos 8:12 tells us that the day will come when *"they shall wander from sea to sea, and from the north even to the east, they shall run to and fro to seek the word of the Lord, and shall not find it."*

Some people believe that when the anti-Christ comes, he will have the authorities take away all our Bibles as the medieval church did back in the dark ages. But think of what an impossible task that would be! No, the authorities are not going to come and take our Bibles away, but there are multitudes of people who will not study for themselves, and at best, will only listen to what preachers and teachers have to say.

When preachers and teachers speak with a lot of *dark speech* and people do not ask, *"What does that mean?"* or will not put forth an effort to learn the meaning themselves, they will not <u>know</u> the Word of the Lord. Thus, in a sense, the Word will be taken away even though they hold the Bible in their hands!

We must know the Word, follow the Word, and be careful to confirm, from the Word, the teachings of others. Note carefully these words written long ago:

"Christ had many truths to give to His disciples, of which He could not speak, because they did not advance with the light that was flashed upon the Levitical laws and the sacrificial offerings. They did not embrace the light, advance with the light, and follow on to still greater brightness as Providence should lead the way.

And for the same reason Christ's disciples of 1897 do not comprehend important matters of truth. So dull has been the comprehension of even those who teach the truth to others that many things cannot be opened to them until they reach heaven. It ought not to be so.... They close their minds as though there were no more for them to learn, and should the Lord attempt to lead them on, they would not take up with the increased light....

The development of truth will be the reward to the humble-hearted seeker, who will fear God and walk with Him" (Ellen G. White Estate, Inc., *Manuscript Releases Vol. 16*, No. 1201).

The good news is that you and I have a choice. We can take the attitude of a servant and cling to the dark speech, murmuring and complaining, *"I don't know why you want me to do that Lord. I don't understand, but I guess for the servant it's not the reason why, but to do or die."*

Or, like Moses, we can be God's friend and ask, *"Lord I really want to understand. Is that really what you said? And Lord, what did you mean when you said that?"* Jesus has promised to help.

In Matthew 7:7, He said, *"Ask, and it shall be given you; seek, and ye shall find."* With all the tools for Bible study available to us today, the commentaries, the Hebrew and Greek dictionaries, and the various versions of the Bible, there is no excuse for us to be in the dark about dark speech.

Let us strive for the deeper understanding we need. It is especially important that we have a clear picture of our heavenly Father and His character, which Jesus went to such great lengths to show us through His life and death as recorded in the Scriptures.

In the next chapter, we will discuss why it is so critical to have the right picture or understanding of God's character.

Chapter Two

OUR PICTURE OF GOD AND
WHY IT IS IMPORTANT

"And this is life eternal, that they might know thee the only true God, and Jesus Christ, whom thou hast sent" (John 17:3).

A critically important doctrine to the church, especially the church of the last days, is the truth about the character of God. This is important for two reasons.

First, knowing the truth about God's character will safeguard us from the worship of false Christs. The Bible says, *"For there shall arise false Christs, and false prophets, and shall shew great signs and wonders; insomuch that, if it were possible, they shall deceive the very elect"* (Matthew 24:24).

Many believe that one day near the end of time, in addition to an anti-Christ appearing as some charismatic, powerful human being who will openly oppose God and rule the world, that Satan himself will appear "in the flesh" claiming to be Christ. As a matter of fact, the word "anti" in the biblical Greek is "antee," which means "in place of." This means that Satan will come claiming to be Christ in place of Christ, thus making Satan himself the real anti-Christ!

Satan, having superhuman powers, will be able to *"show great signs and wonders"* the likes of which the world has never seen. The majority of people in the world will believe that he is Christ as he claims, believing that these miraculous things can only come from divine power. So no matter who comes before that, even someone appearing to be a great leader and apparently uniting the world as the anti-Christ is expected to do, ultimately, in

11

the end, Satan will be the one who *"sitteth in the temple of God, shewing himself that he is God"* (2 Thessalonian 2:4). Satan is the ultimate and original anti-Christ!

One point we need to be clear on is that great demonstrations of power and miracles cannot always be trusted as coming from God. Satan can also perform great *signs and wonders*. But what may be more dangerous is that with his superhuman intelligence, he can twist the Scriptures with such subtle deception that he can easily deceive millions into thinking they have the truth when they actually have the lie.

But, and this is important to remember, although Satan can deceive with miracles and words, he cannot perfectly impersonate God's character. And that is what will give him away to those who truly know God and have become His friends. Therefore, only the true knowledge of God's character can be trusted in the last days to discern the true Christ from the false Christ and enable one to recognize the imposter.

Second, and this may be the most important reason; knowing the truth about God's character will have an enormous effect on our own character. The Bible says in Psalms 135:15-18, *"The idols of the heathen are silver and gold, the work of men's hands. They have mouths, but they speak not; eyes have they, but they see not; they have ears, but they hear not; neither is there any breath in their mouths. They that make them are like unto them: so is every one that trusteth in them."*

Did you catch the point in this passage? Those who make the idols and those who trust in the idols will become <u>like</u> the idols! This does not mean that a person will become a statue of brass or granite as those idols were, but it does mean that the person who worships the idol will develop a character like the idol is believed to have.

There is a natural and spiritual law that says "by beholding we will become changed into the same image." That is, a person will begin to copy and eventually develop the character and values of the idol, celebrity, or god they revere and worship. This is the "Law of Worship."

One example of this human trait is seen in the way most teens relate to popular movie or rock stars, which ironically are often referred to as "idols." As the kids become devoted fans of these celebrities, they begin to dress like them, talk like them, and attempt to be like them in every way possible.

This same principle applies to the worship of God as well. Note the following verse: *"But we all, with open face beholding as in a glass the glory of the Lord, are changed into the same image from glory to glory, even as by the Spirit of the Lord"* (2 Corinthians 3:18).

This verse is basically saying that by beholding the glory of the Lord a person is changed into the same image by the work of the Holy Spirit. *"Beholding"* means to observe, to contemplate, to meditate upon. In this case, a person beholding the Lord would not become omnipotent (all powerful), omniscient (all knowing), and omnipresent (everywhere at once) as God is, but they would begin to develop the same nature or character as the Lord. They would truly come to be like Jesus!

You will notice the text says that by *"beholding the glory of the Lord."* What is the glory of the Lord referring to? If we go back to the story of Moses, we find he once asked the Lord to show him His glory:

> "And he [Moses] said, I beseech thee, shew me thy glory. And he [the Lord] said, I will make all my goodness pass before thee, and I will proclaim the name of the LORD before thee; and will be gracious to whom I will be gracious, and will shew mercy on whom I will shew mercy. And he [the Lord] said, Thou canst not see my face: for there shall no man see me, and live.
>
> And the LORD said, Behold, there is a place by me, and thou shalt stand upon a rock: And it shall come to pass, while my glory passeth by, that I will put thee in a clift of the rock, and will cover thee with my hand while I pass by: And I will take away mine hand, and

thou shalt see my back parts: but my face shall not be seen" (Exodus 33:18-23).

Notice when Moses asked to see His glory, the Lord said, *"I will make all my goodness pass before thee."* The Lord put Moses in the cleft of the rock and then the Bible says, *"And the LORD passed by before him, and proclaimed, The LORD, The LORD God, merciful and gracious, long-suffering, and abundant in goodness and truth, keeping mercy for thousands, forgiving iniquity and transgression and sin"* (Exodus 34:6, 7).

The glory of the Lord that God wanted Moses to see was not His form or His awesome power, but rather the *glory* of His gracious character! His gracious character is what He wants us to behold today so that we may be changed into His image and be more like Him.

For example, because of our inherited selfish nature, we would not naturally think of loving our enemies. The human nature compels us to hate our enemy. But as we study the Bible, Jesus tells us that we are to forgive and love our enemies. And more than just telling us what we should do, He demonstrated it by forgiving, loving, and dying for his enemies.

Reading about Christ's example, it awakens something good in us, and He empowers us to love our enemies too! He is our model of true righteousness. If we are going to idolize a man, it should be the *Jesus Christ* who is the perfect representation of the character of God Himself, being the *"express image of His person"* (Hebrews 1:3).

So we have two distinct choices before us. One is to behold some worldly idol, person, or system, and become worldly, or we can behold Jesus and become like Him! However, don't forget the lesson in the previous chapter. If, because of misunderstanding or dark speech, we develop a false picture of God, we will, in a sense, be worshiping a false god.

One thoughtful Bible commentator made the following insightful statement: *"Multitudes have a wrong con-*

ception of God and his attributes, and are as truly serving a false god as were the worshipers of Baal" (Review and Herald, November 6, 1913).

Does this statement help you to see why our picture of God is so critical? What makes the worship of a false god so dangerous for us is that we will develop the character of the god we worship. In the case of the Christian, if we see God as rigid, harsh, angry with sinners, punishing them, and condemning them, then we will likely become rigid, harsh Christians who judge and condemn others whom we see as sinners (forgetting we are sinners too)!

You may recall that Jesus said the day would come when *"whosoever killeth you will think that he doeth God service"* (John 16:2). Note that these are religious people doing this, thinking it to be a service to God! John 16:3 tells us why they do this: *"And these things they will do unto you, because they have not known the Father, nor me."*

They do this because of their misunderstanding of God's nature, believing He would approve of such conduct! They believe that they are simply His instruments to carry out His will. Does the church today see God in this light? Is He seen as an executioner of the wicked? If so, what effect will that have on our character and how we look at those whom we see as hopeless sinners? Keep this question in mind as we continue our study.

So how do we know we are beholding the true God and not some false image? How do we know we have the right picture of God? We do that by laying aside our pride, our preconceived ideas and opinions, and go to God's Word *as little children* with an open, inquisitive mind.

As we go through the Bible, we will find different pictures of God. We see a God who drowned the world in the flood, a God who came down in fire and flame and thundered on Mt. Sinai, a God who consumed Nadab and Abihu with fire, a God who ordered the stoning of

Achan and his family, and a God who rained fire down from heaven on Mt. Carmel. We see a fearful picture of an awesome deity not to be trifled with.

Do you think God enjoyed doing those terrible things we read about Him doing in the Old Testament? Parents, do you enjoy disciplining your children, especially when it requires punishment? But which shows the greater love, to refuse to discipline your child because you fear he will fear you and hate you or run the risk of being feared and thought badly of in order to properly train the child for his own good?

The Lord is not willing to let his children perish uninstructed and unwarned, so He ran the risk of intervening in the lives of man, and Satan has taken advantage of that to make God look like a tyrant.

There is a real danger of the Bible reader becoming preoccupied with the fearful pictures of God in Scripture and overlooking the other pictures that are there. While it is true that there can be seen a God of wrath, there can also be seen the picture of God as a loving Father who is unbelievably patient with His disobedient and rebellious children. We can see a loving God who blesses and provides for the just and the unjust, the good and the evil.

There is no denying these contrasts are in the Bible. Are we to accept the ones we like and disregard the rest? No, that would be being dishonest with the Scriptures. We must find the balance between these two contrasting pictures to find the truth.

If you had a medical book that only had the pictures and descriptions of the deadly effects of disease in it, it would not be very helpful. It would be an ugly and frightening book. On the other hand, if that medical book had not only the pictures and description of the effects of disease, but also the treatment and cure for disease, then it would be a helpful book, a good book.

In the same way, if we only look at the pictures of God in the Bible that show Him exercising wrath and vengeance in emergency situations, we may see a harsh and wrathful God. But in the Bible, we not only have the ugly record of the disease of sin and how God has had to deal with a rebellious, sinful people, we also have a record of a loving God who has demonstrated He has the cure for the disease of sin and is working patiently and compassionately to reach and save everyone He can. This makes the Bible the good book that ultimately reveals and vindicates the character of God.

For a better understanding of this complicated issue, I highly recommend the book *Who Is Afraid of the Old Testament God* by Alden Thompson.

Having said all of that, there are still those who, in a sense, see two different Gods in the Bible and thus divide the Trinity. First, they see the God of the Old Testament as the Father God, severe, arbitrary, wrathful, and unforgiving. Then they see God's Son, Jesus, in the New Testament as gentle and merciful, kind and compassionate, not at all like the Father. They have been told the Son must plead with the Father to forgive us as though the Father were reluctant to grant pardon to the sinner, demanding justice for His broken law.

However, there is a problem with this viewpoint when we consider that Jesus plainly stated, *"I and my Father are one"* (John 10:30). Any teaching that portrays the Father and Son as not being in total, complete harmony and union with one another, separates the Trinity, and is erroneous. These kinds of errors continue to cloud our picture of God.

In the next chapter, we will take another look at the Trinity in a way that will hopefully reveal a better understanding of this complex subject.

Chapter Three

UNDERSTANDING THE TRINITY

"But the Comforter, which is the Holy Ghost, whom the Father will send in my name, he shall teach you all things, and bring all things to your remembrance, whatsoever I have said unto you" (John 14:26).

We have evidence that there are three persons in the Godhead because of verses like John 14:26: *"But the Comforter, which is the Holy Ghost* [one person], *whom the Father* [a second person] *will send in my name, he shall teach you all things, and bring all things to your remembrance, whatsoever I* [Jesus, a third person] *have said unto you."*

It is easily seen there are three persons in this verse, the Holy Spirit, the Father, and the Son, Jesus. The three persons of the Godhead are co-eternal, co-divine, and co-equal, that is, they are all God. They all have existed from eternity, and one does not have authority or rank over the other. They are as one, in perfect harmony and unity of purpose and character. As a matter of fact, anywhere you find the name Father or Son or Holy Spirit, you can substitute one name—God.

God is infinite, limitless in power, time, and space. It is impossible for mankind, with his limited mental abilities, to grasp all that God is. But to help His finite (limited) creatures better understand His divine nature and enter into a relationship with Him, the three members of the Godhead have taken different roles upon themselves.

One member of the Godhead has assumed the role of the Father. The Father is understood as the omnipotent, all-powerful, Almighty God seated on the throne in heaven. He is the One who is in control, directing the affairs of the universe. He is the One who is *"dwelling in light which no man can approach unto"* (I Timothy 6:16). He is the One who knows everything, seeing *"the end from the beginning"* (Isaiah 46:10). The Father is reigning from His position, seated on the throne in heaven, continuously from eternity past to eternity future, forever and ever.

The Bible teaches that God is omnipresent. That means He is ever-present, everywhere, all the time. It is difficult for man, with his limited mind, to comprehend how God's presence can be everywhere in the universe at the same time and still be seen as One seated on the throne too.

This is where another person of the Godhead comes in. He takes the role of the Spirit, the One who is understood as being everywhere and invisible, who impresses the mind with truth. The Spirit is the teacher and helper who, instead of sitting on the throne in heaven, sits on the throne in the hearts of believers.

Finally, humanity needed to see God in a visual way, to see *"God with flesh on"* so to speak, to see how He would act if He were one of them. This is the role of the Son, the One who came *"in the flesh"* to give us a clearer picture of what God is really like. The Son, in this role, is also the Intermediary. As 1 Timothy 2:5 says, *"For there is one God, and one mediator between God and men, the man Christ Jesus."*

Jesus is God in the flesh. That means that God in the person of Jesus Christ is our Intercessor. Since it is impossible for us to go to heaven to learn about God, we needed someone to bring Him down to us, to serve as a connection (intercessor/mediator) between God and us. Jesus Christ is the one in the Godhead that brings God down to us and makes that connection possible.

The Son is unique. He is *"Jacob's ladder,"* the link between heaven and earth, between God and man. And just as the person of the Father remains on the throne, and the person of the Holy Spirit remains the invisible guide in the heart, so the person of the Son remains as the intermediary, the one and only link between heaven and earth. Either as a man among us (Immanuel) or as our High Priest in the heavenly sanctuary (Hebrews 8:1), He has been in this role from the beginning. Note the following text:

> "Who is the image of the invisible God, the firstborn of every creature: For by Him were all things created, that are in heaven, and that are in earth, visible and invisible, whether they be thrones, or dominions, or principalities, or powers: all things were created by him and for him: And he is before all things, and by him all things consist. And he is the head of the body, the church" (Colossians 1:15-18).

In this passage, did you notice the following? (1) He is the image of the invisible God: One that could be seen; (2) He is the Creator, as well as Savior; and (3) He is the head of the church. Jesus, the Son, is all this.

He is the Lord God we read of in the Old Testament. His voice was the voice of God that spoke and the earth was created; His hands were the hands of God that formed man from the dust of the earth. He was the God who walked with Adam and Eve in the cool of the evening in the Garden of Eden. He was the God who appeared to Moses in the burning bush. He was *"the angel of the Lord"* who led Israel through the wilderness in a pillar of cloud by day and a pillar of fire by night. He was the God who came down on Mt. Sinai in fire and flame and gave the commandments.

For clear evidence of this, compare the previous text, *"For by Him were all things created, that are in heaven, and that are on earth,"* with Nehemiah 9:6, which says, "Thou, even thou, art LORD alone; thou hast made heaven, *the heaven of heavens, with all their host, the earth, and all things that are therein, the seas, and all that is therein, and thou preservest them all; and the host of heaven worshippeth thee."*

Who is this speaking of? According to what we just read in Colossians, it is the Son of God, the pre-incarnate Christ. Nehemiah continues in verse 7-13:

> "Thou art the LORD the God, who didst choose Abram, and broughtest him forth out of Ur of the Chaldees, and gavest him the name of Abraham; And foundest his heart faithful before thee, and madest a covenant with him to give the land of the Canaanites, the Hittites, the Amorites, and the Perizzites, and the Jebusites, and the Girgashites, to give it, I say, to his seed, and hast performed thy words; for thou art righteous:
>
> And didst see the affliction of our fathers in Egypt, and heardest their cry by the Red sea; And showedst signs and wonders upon Pharaoh, and on all his servants, and on all the people of his land: for thou knewest that they dealt proudly against them. So didst thou get thee a name, as it is this day. And thou didst divide the sea before them, so that they went through the midst of the sea on the dry land; and their persecutors thou threwest into the deeps, as a stone into the mighty waters. Moreover thou leddest them in the day by a cloudy pillar; and in the night by a pillar of fire, to give them light in the way wherein they should go.
>
> Thou camest down also upon mount Sinai, and spakest with them from heaven, and gavest them right judgments, and true laws, good statutes and commandments."

Again, who did all this? The same One who created all things: the Son of God. Ephesians 3:9 clearly states, *"And to make all men see what is the fellowship of the mystery, which from the beginning of the world hath been hid in God, who created all things by Jesus Christ."*

In the preceding texts it can be clearly seen, the Son, whom we know best as Jesus, was the Creator and Lord God of the Old Testament as well as the Savior of the New Testament. Jesus gave up His equal position with the Father on the throne and came and lived with men, as a man. He suffered and struggled with the human race from creation, and when the time was right, He walked among us so that we could see, touch, and talk to Him. He then died on the cross and arose the third day.

All this was in the Father's plan, carried out by the Son, impressed on our hearts and minds by the Holy Spirit, and witnessed by the angels.

The Holy Trinity is One God. Jesus said, *"He that hath seen me hath seen the Father"* (John 14:9). In other words, the Father is just like me!

Then Jesus said, *"And I will pray the Father, and he shall give you another Comforter"* (John 14:16). The *Comforter* referred to here is the Holy Spirit. The word *"another"* is translated from the Greek word *"allos"* meaning *"of the same kind."*

In other words, Jesus is saying that the Holy Spirit, whom the Father will send to be your comforter and helper, is just like Me! I am just like the Father and the Holy Spirit is just like Me. We are all the same; We are One!

The words Jesus spoke are stunning when we truly comprehend what Jesus is saying when He said, *"he that hath seen me hath seen the Father"* (John 14:9).

Do you realize the impact of this statement? Jesus is saying, *"If you have seen me, you have seen God! God is just like me!"* The Trinity cannot be separated. If the Father had come instead of the Son, it would have made no difference. God is not what His enemies have made Him out to be—God is just like Jesus! That is good news! That is the everlasting gospel!

I hope this brief study has given you a better understanding of the Trinity. As I mentioned in the last chapter, it is sad that some have pictured the Son and the Father at odds with each other, with the Son having to plead with the Father and persuade Him to forgive His erring children. Maybe worse is the fact that there are some religions today that, while claiming to believe in God, do not accept the truth that Jesus is God, and thus do not accept the doctrine of the Trinity.

The tragedy is that, in rejecting this truth, they have no accurate picture of God. Without Jesus, we cannot really know what God is like and how He would act if He were human like us. We would have no divine-human model to pattern our lives after. As we discussed in the previous chapter, without the true picture of God we see in Christ, men will more than likely develop a false picture of God and thus be in danger of worshipping a false god. And when they worship a false god, they become like that false god instead of becoming like Jesus.

I believe this is one reason for the history of violence we have seen in many religions, including Christianity. Unfortunately, violence in the name of God continues today, even in our so-called enlightened society. But think of it, if everyone saw God as being just like Jesus, it would be difficult for them to find a place for violence against another, even an enemy.

Satan lied about God in heaven; Satan lied about God in the Garden of Eden; and Satan has lied about God in the church! Satan is continually misrepresenting the character of God to humanity. Years ago, I saw a large sign hanging in a kids' Sabbath School room in the Atlanta Belvedere Seventh-day Adventist Church. It said, "Don't get your facts from the snake!" Good advice! We must be careful we aren't getting our facts from Satan, the "snake."

We have a perfect photograph of God, and that is Jesus Christ. Jesus came to reveal what the Father, who is so often misunderstood and lied about, is really like. That is the reason God couldn't send an angel to do the work Jesus did. An angel simply could not fully portray the character of God. Only God could do that.

I believe one of the things that has done much to blur our picture of God in the Christian church is what I will refer to as the "legal model" of the plan of salvation. In the next chapter, we will begin to examine this model, and how, through dark speech and a distorted picture of

God, many Christians have a false concept of what God is like and how He saves sinners.

Chapter Four

INTRODUCING THE LEGAL MODEL

"In every thing give thanks: for this is the will of God in Christ Jesus concerning you. Quench not the Spirit. Despise not prophesyings. Prove all things; hold fast that which is good" (1 Thessalonians 5:18-21).

The Bible tells us to *"prove* [test] *all things."* The purpose of the next two chapters is to test, or examine, the current traditional understanding of the biblical plan of salvation. This understanding has been prevalent in Christian denominations for centuries and is usually expressed or explained using forensic or court room metaphors and language. Because of that, we will refer to this traditional model as the "legal model."

Before we proceed, I think it is important that we define the words, legal, law, and forensic, so that we are clear on their meaning. Following are the basic definitions as they are found in *Webster's English Dictionary*:

- The word "legal" is defined as: (1) relating to law, or (2) deriving authority from, or founded on, law.

- The word "law" is defined as: (1) A rule of conduct recognized by formal enactment, which a community considers as binding upon its members, or (2) A rule of conduct having divine origin.

- The word "forensic" is defined as: (1) pertaining to courts of justice, or (2) relating to or used in legal proceedings.

When many Christians hear the word legal, they immediately think of legalism. However, I do not refer to this as a legal model because it is a salvation-by-works model, but rather because it is modeled after the forensic, court-room scenario with its legal methods and terminology.

In this chapter, we will highlight what I believe is the origin of the traditional legal model of salvation and list seven of its key points. Then in the next chapter, we will investigate each point for any possible shortcoming.

I realize the things that we will examine here are very precious to many sincere Christians, and I do not take this lightly. I do not wish to begin by stating that this model is wrong. My question is this: Is this model all we need, or is there a better model that more clearly represents the true character of God and the plan of salvation?

As those living in the closing hours of earth's history, I believe these are legitimate questions, and only an honest investigation of this model will help us find the answers. If the traditional legal model in the church today is the best model, it will bear up under close scrutiny and those who place their faith in it have nothing to fear. If it can't, the honest Christian certainly needs to know that.

So let's begin. I think we can, with a fair amount of certainty, trace this model as far back as the Apostle Paul, who wrote the largest portion of the New Testament. In some of his epistles or writings, Paul used legal meta-phors and language. The book of Romans, with his heavy use of law, is a prime example. However, when an illus-tration, metaphor, or model is taken beyond its intended purpose, error can be the result.

I believe this is the reason it would be beneficial for us to examine the traditional model of the plan of salvation carefully to determine if that is the case. If we find that it is the case, and if we find there is a better model, the church would certainly benefit from that knowledge.

As I mentioned, Paul made use of a legal model in his writings, speaking often of "law." The legal scenario and terminology used by Paul illustrated points to the primary audience he was addressing in some of his letters. They were familiar with legal matters of law and could relate to this approach. But, I believe it is doubtful that Paul intended this legal metaphor to be carried over into or dominate every doctrine on salvation. As a matter of fact, some other books of the New Testament contain little, if any, *legal* terminology at all.

Something else that contributed to using legal metaphors and language in religion took place during the period in history called the Dark Ages. This time period was called the Dark Ages because it was during this period that common people had little, if any, access to the Bible.

Without the light of God's Word and wisdom, many philosophical (human) teachings that had no biblical basis were established in the church. This resulted in a corrupt religious system that, united with the power of the state, persecuted and executed millions. Corruption and violence in the church led many to call for reform. Leading out in the reformation movement were gifted leaders like William Tyndale, John Wycliffe, John Huss, Martin Luther, John Calvin, and others, whom it appeared God was guiding back to the truths of His Word.

Soon the cry "sola scriptura," the Latin slogan for "the Bible and the Bible only," was to become the cry of the Reformation. To great numbers of people, the teachings of these men, especially Luther and Calvin, were seen as authoritative, and eventually, church denominations were founded around them. For example, the Lutheran Church was founded on much of Luther's doctrine, and the Presbyterian Church was formed based on the teachings of Calvin.

Calvin, who had a brilliant mind, studied law in Paris. Years later, he decided to enter the ministry even though he was trained as a lawyer, not a theologian. In spite of this background, orthodox Christianity chose to base many of its doctrines (beliefs/teachings) on the writings of Calvin.

During the Great Reformation period, Calvin wrote a monumental four-volume work titled The Institutes of the Christian Religion. The beginning of this work commenced in AD 1535 and reached its final form in AD 1559. Calvin's teachings contained in these volumes have had an enormous impact on many major church bodies to this day. The doctrine of the immortality of the soul, the eternal suffering of the lost in hellfire, and predestination are a few that can be traced back to Calvin's influence on the church through this work.

The King James Version of the Bible was translated during this period (AD 1611), and it appears that its translators may have been influenced by the writings of Calvin as well. The evidence of that can be seen in the use of many Latin based, legal words such as justification, sanctification, and propitiation. These words were not the words of Paul or Peter or John, since their original manuscripts were written in Greek, not in Latin. Latin is the language heavily used even to this day in the legal profession and preferred by Calvin.

Words grounded in the legal system such as law, judgment, justice, justification, sanctification, and propitiation are all from the "legal" Latin. It should come as no surprise that we find a lot of this legal terminology prevalent in this most popular and widely accepted version of the Bible and thus in church teachings.

I believe that the things we have discussed here played a major role in the development of the traditional legal model of the plan of salvation believed and taught by so many in the church today.

Below are seven key points of the traditional legal model. Please understand that there are variations of this model, but the following points are pretty much held in common in most all of them.

First point—God is the sovereign supreme ruler and Creator of all things, in heaven and earth.

Second point—God, being Creator of the universe, has the right and thus has established His law as He has seen fit in order to regulate both nature and govern the behavior of men and angels.

Third point—God, being the law giver, has also determined the penalty for violation of His law. The penalty includes suffering, pain, and death, with the ultimate and final penalty, referred to as the second death.

Fourth point—God, being the Creator and law giver, rightly holds the position of judge and executioner of the sentence against the violators of His law. He has set a future judgment day when He will determine who will be granted eternal life and who He will be sentenced to the second death and be cast into the lake of fire.

Fifth point—The Almighty God is a loving God, but He is also just. By this it is meant that He must see to it that those guilty of breaking His law pay the full penalty due. In order for humans guilty of violating God's law to be released from the penalty, God must forgive them. Because He is just, He cannot simply forgive sinners without the penalty being paid, so He sent His Son to take the sinner's place and suffer the penalty by dying on the cross. This is seen as enabling God to forgive the sinner and still be just. However, even though Jesus has paid the penalty in full, pardon is granted only on the basis of a person's acceptance or belief in the sacrifice of Jesus on their behalf.

Sixth Point—Upon acceptance of, or faith in, Christ's sacrifice, which provides for the forgiveness of sins, a person will be declared not guilty in the judgment and ushered into the gates of paradise, but a person's rejection of God's love and forgiveness will bring forth God's wrath with a verdict of guilty, and they will be *cast into the lake of fire*.

Seventh Point—Whether one is ushered into the gates of paradise or the lake of fire, the results are eternal.

After viewing these basic points in the legal model, it should be easy for one to see that <u>the main objective of the legal model is forgiveness, or, to use the legal word, pardon</u>. If a person can be forgiven, they will not have to suffer God's wrath and the awful experience of the judgment and second death but will enjoy the eternal bliss of the heavenly paradise.

In the next chapter, we will examine each one of these points by using the Bible and logic. Through our study, we will either confirm each one or determine if perhaps we need to take a closer look at the validity of a particular point.

Chapter Five

A CLOSER LOOK AT THE LEGAL MODEL

"Study to shew thyself approved unto God, a workman that needeth not to be ashamed, rightly dividing the word of truth" (2 Timothy 2:15).

In this chapter, we will begin taking each one of the seven key points of the legal model of the plan of salvation listed in the previous chapter and examine them closely using the Bible and logic or common sense as our guide. As we conduct our study, we want to either confirm each point or determine if there is something that gives us sufficient reason to question it. As we go through each point, we also want to see how this model reflects the truth about God's character.

First point

God is the sovereign supreme ruler and Creator of all things, in heaven and earth.

Using the Bible as our source of truth, there is no reason to doubt or question this point. God *is* Creator and the supreme sovereign power in the universe. Isaiah 43:10, 11 says, *"Before me there was no God formed, neither shall there be after me. I, even I, am the Lord; and beside me there is no saviour."*

Likewise, Colossians 1:16, 17 declares, *"For by him were all things created, that are in heaven, and that are in earth, visible and invisible, whether they be thrones, or dominions, or principalities, or powers: all things were created by him, and for him: And he is before all things, and by him all things consist."*

33

Second point

God, being Creator of the universe, has the right and thus has established His law as He has seen fit in order to both regulate and govern nature and the behavior of men and angels.

It is clear from the Bible that God as Creator has established principles and laws that govern nature and the behavior of mankind. It is only logical that as the Creator He certainly has the right to do so. The law given on Mt. Sinai by God himself embodies principles that describe the moral behavior God desires of men and women.

The problem is that some religious institutions have taken it upon themselves to change the law of God by taking out some commandments and modifying others. Other religious institutions claim that keeping the law is legalism and declare that the commandments no longer apply to the believer because they have been "nailed to the cross," thereby abolishing them altogether.

All this seems questionable, as well as illogical, when you realize it means that commands such as *"Thou shall not kill"* or *"Thou shall not steal"* could be modified or abolished! Therefore, some discussion may be in order here because of the confusion about how Christians are to relate to God's law.

The key question is: why did God give the law in the first place? Is it that He is arbitrary, that is, demanding that we behave in the way He has chosen for us, for no other reason than just because He said so?

Galatians 3:19 begins with that kind of question: *"Wherefore then serveth the law?"* Then it answers its own question, *"it was added because of transgressions."* In other words, God gave the law because people were behaving in disorderly and harmful ways, hurting themselves and others.

A modern day example would be if people today drove their cars in a safe manner. If everyone always yielded the right of way to other drivers, never drove carelessly or too fast, always stopped at stop signs, and never did anything that would put themselves or others in danger on the roads, would there be any need for the state to legislate laws regulating drivers? No, but we all know it's not that way. Many people drive in a way that is dangerous to themselves and others, so we must have laws to regulate behavior behind the wheel for the good of all.

Now, in the same way, if the people God called out of Egypt loved Him with all their heart and their neighbor as themselves, there would have been no need for God to lay down the law at Mt. Sinai. But, as mentioned previously, the Bible says the people Moses brought out of Egypt were a *stiff-necked* people, meaning they were hard, cruel, severe, obstinate, and difficult.

We can liken God's situation to that of parents who have strong willed, misbehaving children, with whom they must lay down the law in order to bring peace and harmony in the family, not to be arbitrary or show them who is boss, but for the good of the children.

If God is who we believe He is, if He is righteous and all-knowing, if God is love, if God is all this and He says we should do this or that and not do the other, it is not legalism to do what He says. It just makes good sense!

Deuteronomy 6:24 tells us this: *"And the LORD commanded us to do all these statutes, to fear the LORD our God, for our good always, that he might preserve us alive, as it is at this day."* God gave His law for our good always! If that is true, why would anyone want to change it or do away with it as some have done?

Since the Bible clearly says the law was given for our good always, any violation of that law, regardless of who the violator is, will bring suffering and pain to himself or to others. Therefore, we can define sin as rebellion against God's good law of love, love for Him and love for one another. Therefore, this point is valid if understood correctly.

Third point

God, being the law giver, has also determined the penalty for violation of His law. The penalty includes suffering, pain, and death, with the ultimate and final penalty, referred to as the second death.

God, being the Creator of all things, including *principalities and powers*, has established certain principles of law in both the physical and spiritual realms. Having established these laws, there must be a consequence for the violation of these laws; otherwise, they would cease to be law. However, if the law is not seen as arbitrary, how can the penalty be?

The truth is that every action has a sure and certain reaction or consequence. <u>Right</u> actions result in good consequences. <u>Wrong</u> actions result in bad consequences. This, I believe, we all can agree with. The important question is how is God involved in administering the penalty of His violated law? We will discuss this in the next point.

Fourth point

God, being the Creator and law giver, rightly holds the position of judge and executioner of the sentence against the violators of His law. He has set a future judgment day when He will determine who will be granted eternal life and who will be sentenced to the second death and cast into the lake of fire.

We need to examine this point thoughtfully and carefully. Often, I have heard the expression, "God's gonna get you for that!" Many days there seemed to be a dark cloud hanging over me when I knew I had done wrong, wondering what God was going to do to punish me. How many times, when things go badly, have we thought, "I wonder what sin I have committed that God is punishing me this way?"

The book *The Desire of Ages* explains the source of the problem: *"It is true that all suffering results from the transgression of God's law, but this truth had become perverted. Satan, the author of sin and all its results, had led men to look upon disease and death as proceeding from God,—as punishment arbitrarily inflicted on account of sin"* (p. 471).

The important issue we need to come to terms with in this point is this: How is God involved in the execution of the punishment for sin? Is the penalty for sin an arbitrary, externally inflicted punishment as taught by many in the church today? Or, could it be that the punishment for sin, instead of an arbitrary external penalty as we have in our court system, is rather the natural consequence of our actions? The answer to this question will greatly affect our concept of God's character, and that will in turn, ultimately affect our own as well.

As stated in point three, God has established certain principles of law in both the physical and spiritual realm. But, if the law is not arbitrary, then how can the penalty be? It can't. Therefore, we must conclude the penalty is determined by the law of sowing and reaping. Every action has a sure and certain consequence. Right actions will result in good consequences. Wrong actions will result in bad consequences.

Take the law of gravity for example. The law of gravity is God's law. He put it in place for our good. Without it we would all float away. If a person, either ignoring the law of gravity or in defiance of it, jumps out of an airplane at 12,000 feet without a parachute, gravity will pull them rapidly to the ground and the impact will likely kill them. God does not punish this person for breaking His law of gravity. Rather, the punishment comes as the natural consequence of jumping out of the airplane without a parachute.

Do you see the point? God did not punish; the violated law resulted in the painful and deadly penalty.

Just as in the natural realm, so it is in the spiritual realm. There is a certain consequence to the violation of

God's spiritual law which we call "sin." Sin is basically rebellion against what is good and right. The Bible says in James 4:17: *"Therefore to him that knoweth to do good, and doeth it not, to him it is sin."*

When God's law is violated, someone always gets hurt. Sin hurts the one who violated the law as well as the one who was subjected to the violation. And what we often overlook is that in every case, God, who loves us so deeply, is always hurt by our sin.

We may get by for a while, but the Bible says, *"Be sure your sin will find you out"* (Numbers 32:23). Sooner or later the natural consequence of breaking God's good law will come. Galatians 6:7 says, *"Be not deceived; God is not mocked: for whatsoever a man soweth, that will he also reap"*

I believe that long ago God looked into the future and saw that certain types of behavior would result in pain, hatred, disease, and death. God said, these things are evil, don't do these things. Then God looked again and saw certain other types of behavior that brought forth peace, harmony, love, and life. And, God said, these things are right, do these things and live.

I realize this line of thinking may be new to some, but please hear me out. The Bible does say that God *"will by no means clear the guilty"* (Exodus 34:7). But that does not mean that God will personally punish the guilty. It means that God allows the consequences of sin to punish the guilty. Just as the law of gravity, God established the law of sowing and reaping. God will not change this law, but if allowed, God will change the sinner so they can stop their sin, and when sin is stopped, there will be no painful consequences.

As a matter of fact, there are some passages in the Bible that indicate that God does not personally punish the sinner. For example, Psalms 103:10 says, *"He hath not dealt with us after our sins; nor rewarded* [punished] *us according to our iniquities,"* and 2 Corinthians 5:19 says,

"To wit, that God was in Christ, reconciling the world unto himself, not imputing [or counting] *their trespasses unto them."*

These are just a couple of the verses that provide evidence that God does not impose external punishment on the violators of His law because, as we have already discussed, the punishment is the natural consequence or result of the sinful actions. Sin punishes sin!

In James 1:15, the Bible says, *"Then when lust hath conceived, it bringeth forth sin: and sin, when it is finished, bringeth forth death."* Notice that it says it is sin that brings death, not God. It is the natural outworking of the consequences of the continued violation of the law of good.

In the legal model, this concept is rejected or ignored. In the legal model, God is seen as inflicting a legal external punishment against sin. The legal model makes God out to be more feared than sin! I believe we have reason to question the legal model on this point. We will discuss this in more detail in point five.

Finally, the Bible is clear that there will be a future day of judgment when the final consequences of sin and how God is involved will be clearly seen by all. Most importantly, on this day God's name, or character, will be vindicated when everyone receives the final consequences or reward of their choices in life.

Fifth point

The Almighty God is a loving God, but He is also just. By this it is meant that He must see to it that those guilty of breaking His law pay the full penalty due. In order for humans guilty of violating God's law to be released from the penalty, God must forgive them. Because He is just, He cannot simply forgive sinners without the penalty being paid, so He sent His Son to take the sinner's place and suffer the penalty by dying on the cross. This is seen as enabling God to forgive the sinner and still be just.

However, even though Jesus has paid the penalty in full, pardon is granted only on the basis of a person's acceptance of the sacrifice of Jesus on their behalf.

There are some things that we need to think through in this point also. As previously mentioned, the key objective in the legal model is being forgiven by God. Though the statement cannot be found in the Bible, we often read or hear someone say, *"Jesus died so God would forgive us for our sins."*

In a North American Division Church Ministries Bible Study Guide titled *The Perfect Escape*, two statements are made in bold print: "Sin can be forgiven only by death," and "When Jesus died, all our sins were forgiven."

I realize these are comforting words for many Christians, but let's look at this carefully and honestly for what these statements are really saying. This is saying that God requires death before He will forgive, and the death of Jesus met that requirement! That means it must be terribly hard for God to forgive us!

Apparently, some theologians would agree. For example, a professor at Andrews University Theological Seminary in Michigan wrote the following statement in an article titled "The Dynamics of Forgiveness": *"Forgiveness is tough even for God. The sanctuary service teaches us that <u>God cannot forgive without sacrifice</u>"* (http://Error! Hyperlink reference not valid., accessed March 30, 2009).

<u>God cannot forgive without sacrifice</u>? I do not question the faith of those who say these things, but I can't help but wonder if statements such as those previously quoted have been thoroughly and carefully thought through. I wonder if they have considered how God's character is negatively impacted by these comments.

Please follow me carefully on this point. What obviously has not been considered is that statements such as these, though certainly unintended by those who make them, imply that Satan is right, that God (the Father) is not merciful; it is hard for Him to forgive, so hard that in order for Him to forgive He must be appeased with a blood sacrifice.

The sacrifice of animals was not sufficient; they only pointed to what He ultimately required, a human sacrifice, but not just any human, only a perfect, sinless human would suffice! This implies that God must be similar to the ancient pagan gods who also demanded blood sacrifice before they would forgive and bless.

The Bible says that God condemned the practice of the ancient pagans who sacrificed their children to pagan gods, but yet, this view in actuality teaches that God sacrificed His own Son as a propitiation to appease Himself or to atone for what we had done! It is taught that the death of Christ was necessary to satisfy God's justice. Torturing and killing a perfectly innocent man is justice? That makes no sense either! It's no wonder some people are confused about why Jesus had to die.

Now, note carefully what the Bible says in Hosea 6:6: *"For I* [God] *desired mercy, and not sacrifice; and the knowledge of God more than burnt offerings."* And in Psalms 40:6, it states, *"Sacrifice and offering thou didst not desire; mine ears hast thou opened: burnt offering and sin offering hast thou not required."*

Looking in the New Testament, Jesus says, *"But if ye had known what this meaneth, I will have mercy, and not sacrifice, ye would not have condemned the guiltless"* (Matthew 12:7).

These verses clearly say God does not desire or require sacrifice. Why then were they called for in the temple ceremonies? Why does the Bible say, *"Without shedding of blood is no remission"* (Hebrews 9:22)?

Allow me to answer that question with a question. Was the shedding of the blood of a sacrifice, whether it be an animal or the blood of Jesus, necessary <u>to change God</u>? Did the sacrifice cause God to forgive or to love when He would not have done so otherwise? <u>Or</u> was the shedding of blood necessary <u>to change sinners</u>? Was the sacrifice made to break the sinner's hard heart and demonstrate God's love and thus win him back to trust or faith in God?

As bad as it speaks of us as humans, <u>Jesus had to die because there was no other way for God to get through to us</u>. The Bible repeatedly states: God does not change! The blood was shed to change us, to appease us sinful rebels, not God. To reconcile us back to God, not God back to us. How wonderful of God that He was willing to do something this drastic to reach us!

One of my favorite writers, Ellen G. White, states this better than I ever could:

> "The atonement of Christ was not made in order to induce God to love those whom He otherwise hated; and it was not made to produce a love that was not in existence; but it was made as a manifestation of the love that was already in God's heart . . . we are not to entertain the idea that God loves us because Christ has died for us, but that He so loved us that He gave His only-begotten Son to die for us" (*Signs of the Times*, May 30, 1895).

> "God's forgiveness is not merely a judicial act by which He sets us free from condemnation. It is not only forgiveness for sin but reclaiming from sin. It is the outflow of redeeming love that transforms the heart" (*The Faith I Live By*, p. 129).

Another phrase often quoted by the adherents of the legal model is, *"Jesus died to pay for all my sins so I don't have to."* Just as in the previous statement, *"Jesus died so God would forgive us,"* this statement cannot be found in the Bible either.

Think about this: If Jesus died to pay a legal penalty for our sin, and the penalty is to burn in hell for eternity; the penalty is not paid. He's not burning in hell for eternity! If the legal penalty is to suffer as long as we deserve and then be burned alive, the penalty is not paid. He was not burned alive! If the legal penalty is the second death or eternal separation from God, the penalty is not paid, because He was resurrected and is now with the Father!

As we begin to think this through, this point in the legal model presents some serious problems. Again follow me carefully. Christ's death paid for my sins in full. Whether I accept that gift or not does not change the fact that the penalty has been paid. If Christ's death was a *once-and-for-all* legal payment for sin, it would only seem logical that all people would be saved whether they accepted it or not! The debt or penalty has been paid; no further payment or action should be required. The debt no longer exists. Though it may be a wonderful thought, it is not realistic and would never be allowed in any court of law.

The legal model seems to have failed to recognize the difference in civil and criminal law. Civil law permits substitute payment. Your insurance company may pay to repair the damage done by your wrongful act. But criminal law demands that the one who committed the crime pay the penalty for it. Imagine a person guilty of mass murder. As the judge pronounces the death sentence, another person in the courtroom rises and says, "Your Honor, I will die in his place; set him free."

Do you think the judge will allow that? We all know full well no judge in the world would allow that! This type of story has been told many times to illustrate God's pardon of sinners, but this is carrying the legal model to the point of absurdity, far beyond what the Apostle Paul ever intended.

Another problem with this idea is that it detracts from the fact that the suffering of Christ is not to be understood as a onetime legal payment for sin. Rather, Christ is to be seen as *"the Lamb slain from the foundation of the world"* (Revelation 13:8).

This means that Christ has suffered the heart-wrenching agony of the cross, not for one day 2,000 years ago, but every day since sin began, and it hasn't ended yet. Since the first sin in the Garden of Eden, every time a person willfully sins they crucify Christ afresh (Hebrews 6:6)!

Once again, I rely on another writer to word this in just the right way: *"Few give thought to the suffering that sin has caused our Creator. All heaven suffered in Christ's agony; but that suffering did not begin or end with His manifestation in humanity. The cross is a revelation to our dull senses of the pain that, from its very inception, sin has brought to the heart of God. Every departure from the right, every deed of cruelty, every failure of humanity to reach his ideal, brings grief to Him"* (*Education*, p. 263).

Read these words again: *"The cross is a revelation to our dull senses of the pain that, from its very inception, sin has brought to the heart of God." This is what the Bible means when it says Christ was "the Lamb slain from the foundation of the world"* (Revelation 13:8). God has suffered since the very first sin!

Like the song that goes something like this, *"Each time I fail, I swing the hammer that drives the nail,"* He continues to suffer as we continue to willfully sin.

The truth is, Jesus did not die to pay for our sin, nor did He die so that God would forgive us. These legal metaphors cheapen the most magnificent demonstration of love the world will ever see. The cross was the *only way* that God could draw all men to Himself. The cross was the *only way* that God could demonstrate His love in such fashion that men would trust Him again. The cross was the *only way* to expose Satan's lies about God.

As one biblical commentator wrote, *"Without shedding of blood there is no remission for sin. He must suffer the agony of a public death on the cross, that witness of it might be borne without the shadow of a doubt"* (Ellen G. White Estate, Inc., *Manuscript 101*, 1897).

"That witness of it might be borne." In other words, human beings had to see something that dramatic, that shocking, to enable them to see their own sinful, selfish condition in contrast to God's infinite and unselfish love for them.

"In the councils of heaven the cross was ordained as the means of atonement. This was to be God's means of winning men to Him....The Saviour proposed to re-establish the principles of human dependence upon God and cooperation between God and man. He proposed to unite God and man by the golden chain of love" (Ellen G. White Estate, Inc., *Manuscript Releases Vol. 5*, No. 286, p. 114).

This is what Jesus was referring to in John 12:32, 33 when he said, *"And I, if I be lifted up from the earth, will draw all men unto me. This he said, signifying what death he should die."* And this is why Peter wrote in 1 Peter 3:18: *"For Christ also hath once suffered for sins, the just for the unjust, that he might bring us to God, being put to death in the flesh, but quickened by the Spirit."*

Christ sacrificed Himself, not to pay a legal penalty to appease or to change God but to change us, to win us back to trust in God so that God can change us, heal us, save us.

The sinless angels needed the cross too, but not for forgiveness. They had never sinned; they didn't need to be "covered by the blood." Colossians 1:20 says, *"And, having made peace through the blood of his cross, by him to reconcile all things unto himself; by him, I say, whether they be things in earth, or things in heaven."*

Note this thoughtful comment: *"It is through the efficacy* [effectiveness] *of the cross that the angels of heaven are guarded from apostasy. Without the cross, they would be no more secure against evil than were the angels before the fall of Satan. Angelic perfection failed in heaven. Human perfection failed in Eden, the paradise of bliss. All who wish for security in earth or heaven must look to the Lamb of God"* (*Signs of the Times*, September 30, 1889).

Notwithstanding all we have discussed here, the key objective of the legal model remains forgiveness. In that model, the most important question is, "What must I do so that God will forgive me?" But in John 3:3, Jesus says, *"Verily, verily, I say unto thee, Except a man be born again, he cannot see the kingdom of God."*

Let me point out here that Jesus did not say *"except a man be forgiven"* but *"except a man be born again, he cannot see the kingdom of God."* There is a big difference in the two! As important as our need for forgiveness is to relieve us of our guilt, forgiveness will not heal the damage done by sin nor will it save us or alleviate the penalty (more on this in chapter eight).

Our key objective in salvation must be conversion and regeneration, a permanent change of heart and character. There must be a turning away from our selfish, sinful nature and a turning to God for deliverance from and an overcoming of our sin. This is critical.

I am reminded of a story I once heard about Isaiah and King Manasseh. This story is partly true and partly fictitious, but it makes a clear point. The story went something like this: King Manasseh was one of the wickedest kings that ever reigned over Judah. King Manasseh killed every prophet of God he could get his hands on. One day, he captured the prophet Isaiah, put him in a hollow log and sawed him in half, killing him. The moment Isaiah died, he entered into the state of unconsciousness the Bible calls "sleep," unaware of what transpired after his death. Isaiah doesn't know that sometime later King Manasseh was touched by the Holy Spirit and converted.

On resurrection day, they both are awakened at the Lord's coming and taken to heaven. One day, Isaiah is walking down the streets of gold, turns a corner and lo and behold, he sees none other than King Manasseh, and he has a saw in his hand! (He was going to trim one of the bushes outside his mansion). Isaiah, remembering what the king did to him, runs to the Lord and says, "Lord, do you know who I just saw? I just saw King Manasseh, and he has a saw! Lord, what is he doing here? Lord, you re-member what he did!" And the Lord says to Isaiah, "Oh, it's OK, Isaiah, I forgave him." (Original story told by A. Graham Maxwell.)

Is that very comforting to Isaiah? No, Isaiah wants to know that Manasseh has a new heart and a right spirit. He wants to know that he is a changed man who would never think of doing those things again.

Do you see the problem with this point in the legal model? Simply being forgiven does not heal the damage done. It does little to change the heart or the character, and that change is what is absolutely necessary for sal-vation to be accomplished. (Again, for a more detailed study of forgiveness, see chapter eight).

Sixth Point

Upon acceptance of, or faith in, Christ's sacrifice pro-viding the forgiveness of sins, a person will be declared not guilty in the judgment and ushered into the gates of paradise, but a person's rejection of God's love and for-giveness will bring forth God's wrath with a verdict of guilty at which time they will be *cast into the lake of fire.*

According to the legal model, forgiveness is only granted on the basis of acceptance of the sacrifice of Jesus Christ in our place. There are those who declare that all that is necessary is to *only believe, "Jesus has done it all."* However, others disagree. Note the following statement:

> "There are many who view themselves as defective in character when they look into God's moral mirror, His law; but they have heard so much of 'all you have to do is to believe, only believe that Jesus has done it all, and you have nothing to do in the matter,' that after venturing to look into the mirror they straightway go from it retaining all their defects, with the words on their lips, 'Jesus has done it all'" (Review and Herald, October 11, 1887).

The truth is that if I believe the gospel and that Jesus died for me, and that belief does not motivate me to surrender my heart to God, thus cooperating with Him to bring about a change for the good in my heart and life, then my believing is useless. It will only lead to presumption.

Presumption is another danger with the legal model because of so much emphasis on forgiveness. Many think that because they are forgiven, they are saved no matter how they live from that point on. The "once saved, always saved" doctrine may have grown out of this idea. But even though a person is truly forgiven, if there is no real change in their heart and life, they are still in their sins and are still lost.

At the same time, let me say this: considering that so many people picture God as judge and executioner, they need this legal model that they may have assurance of forgiveness and an escape from His wrath. They are comforted believing that Jesus, as their advocate or lawyer, is interceding between them and God and that He is pleading His blood to appease the Father's anger. It may be that this is God's way of reaching these people where they are until they are open to a better understanding.

Understanding that, the legal model may have its purpose in God's overall plan, but as we closely and honestly examine it point by point, there is reason for concern. The Trinity is divided against itself with the Son pleading with the Father to accept and forgive us. Furthermore, there is more emphasis on forgiveness than regeneration, and God's character is distorted, which may be the greatest problem. I believe we must conclude that it may not be the ideal model for Christians today.

When referencing today's church, you may have heard someone use the word "progressive," which means "to progress" or "to grow." The church is to *grow in grace, and in the knowledge of our Lord and Saviour Jesus Christ"* (2 Peter 3:18).

The church can't grow if it does not learn more about our infinite, unchangeable, and gracious God. We can't put God in a box and say, "that is all there is." God is limitless and there is so much more for us to learn about Him and His ways.

Isaiah 55:8, 9 says, *"For my thoughts are not your thoughts, neither are your ways my ways, saith the LORD. For as the heavens are higher than the earth, so are my ways higher than your ways, and my thoughts than your thoughts."*

We must begin to think outside the box of human understanding. We must be careful we do not create God in our image, but that we are restored to His.

Seventh Point

Whether one is ushered into the gates of paradise or cast into the lake of fire, the results are eternal. On this point the Bible is clear; the consequences of the choices we make in life are eternal. However, there are many variations of what the Bible means when it speaks of eternal life or eternal death. In the legal model, these are seen as a reward or punishment. But there is much more to it. Even if there is no heaven or hell, if this life is all there is, God's way of unselfish love is the best way to live.

After the investigation of these points, my question remains. Is the legal model all we need? Is there a better model that more clearly represents the true character of God and the plan of salvation? Do we have such a model that can be supported by Scripture? The answer is yes, I believe we do, and we will introduce that model in the next chapter.

Chapter Six

INTRODUCING THE HEALING MODEL

"For this people's heart is waxed gross, and their ears are dull of hearing, and their eyes they have closed; lest at any time they should see with their eyes, and hear with their ears, and should understand with their heart, and should be converted, and I should heal them" (Matthew 13:15).

In the previous chapter, we examined seven key points of the traditional, legal model of the plan of salvation. As we studied, we found that some points were questionable. We closed the chapter with the suggestion that there may be a better model of the plan of salvation. In this chapter, I will introduce what I believe to be a better metaphor for understanding sin and God's way of saving people. We will refer to this model as the "healing model."

In the healing model, sin is not seen as the breaking of a rule of law or code of conduct for which an external punishment will be rendered similar to the judicial system. The sinner is not seen as a criminal deserving of punishment for his crimes. Rather, in this model, sin is seen as an infection of the heart and mind, a sickness, an inherited terminal illness, that, if not cured, will cause suffering and eventually the death of its victim as a natural consequence of the infection itself.

In this model, God is not seen as the judge and executioner, but rather as the Great Physician who only is able to cure this deadly sickness and restore its victims to perfect health and ultimately eternal life.

Before I begin to list the various points of this model and examine them as we did those of the legal model, I think it is important that we confirm that this model has a scriptural foundation.

Following are two verses that depict the plan of salvation in a healing model or metaphor: *"I said, LORD, be merciful to me; heal my soul, for I have sinned against thee"* (Psalms 41:4), and *"Heal me, O LORD, and I shall be healed; save me, and I shall be saved"* (Jeremiah 17:14).

These two verses are written in a style known as Hebrew poetry. Instead of ending each sentence with words that rhyme as we do in English, in Hebrew poetry, the second part of the sentence explains, clarifies, or restates what is said in the first part. The writers of both of the previous verses are stating that being saved is like being healed.

In Isaiah 53:5, the prophet writes, *"But he was wounded for our transgressions, he was bruised for our iniquities; the chastisement for our peace was upon him, and by his stripes we are healed."*

"By His stripes we are healed." Common sense tells us that His suffering does not cure physical disease, but it does draw us to Him. And in so doing, it leads to recovery from or healing of the sin-sick soul. As a matter of fact, the Greek word translated "wicked" can also mean "diseased".

Most Christians are familiar with the New Testament term for salvation, the English word *"saved,"* which is translated from the Greek word *"sozo,"* meaning *"to be well,"* *"to be whole,"* or *"to be safe or saved."*

The translators of the King James Version Bible translated it with all three meanings. Note the following examples:

- *"My little daughter lieth at the point of death: I pray thee, come and lay thy hands on her, that she may be healed [sozo]"* (Mark 5:23).

- *"For she said, If I may touch but his clothes, I shall be whole* [sozo]." (Mark 5:28).

- *"It is easier for a camel to go through the eye of a needle, than for a rich man to enter into the kingdom of God. And they were astonished out of measure, saying among themselves, Who then can be saved* [sozo]?" (Mark 10:25, 26).

These three English words—saved, healed, whole— are all translated from the same Greek word, sozo. So when referring to our salvation, we could say, *"I am healed"* or *"I am made whole,"* instead of saying, *"I am saved."*

As seen in the following examples in the New Testament, Jesus used the healing metaphor many times to illustrate salvation.

"They that are whole have no need of the physician, but they that are sick: I came not to call the righteous, but sinners to repentance" (Mark 2:17).

In this verse, Jesus likens the sinner to the sick who need a physician, who need healing. *"For this people's heart is waxed gross, and their ears are dull of hearing, and their eyes they have closed; lest at any time they should see with their eyes, and hear with their ears, and should understand with their heart, and should be converted, and I should heal them"* (Matthew 13:15).

The Greek word *"heal"* in this verse has only one meaning and that is *"to cure."* Jesus is not referring to physical healing in this verse but rather spiritual healing of the sin-sick soul.

"For whether is easier, to say, Thy sins be forgiven thee; or to say, Arise, and walk? But that ye may know that the Son of man hath power on earth to forgive sins, (then saith he to the sick of the palsy,) Arise, take up thy bed, and go unto thine house" (Matthew 9:5, 6).

A popular commentary on the life of Christ, *The Desire of Ages*, emphasizes spiritual healing in commenting on this passage:

> "It required nothing less than creative power to restore health to that decaying body. The same voice that spoke life to man created from the dust of the earth had spoken life to the dying paralytic. And the same power that gave life to the body had renewed the heart. He who at the creation "spake, and it was," who "commanded, and it stood fast," (Ps. 33:9), had spoken life to the soul dead in trespasses and sins. The healing of the body was an evidence of the power that had renewed the heart. Christ bade the paralytic arise and walk, "that ye may know," He said, "that the Son of man hath power on earth to forgive sins."
>
> The paralytic found in Christ healing for both the soul and the body. The spiritual healing was followed by physical restoration. This lesson should not be overlooked" (p. 269).

Another book, *Counsels on Health*, clearly uses the healing model metaphor when comparing the spiritual and physical health: *"Christ came as the Great Physician to heal the wounds that sin has made in the human family, and His Spirit, working through His servants, imparts to sin-sick, suffering human beings a mighty healing power that is efficacious for the body and the soul"* (p. 210).

Another insightful statement is found in a letter written in 1906 and found in the *S.D.A. Bible Commentary, Vol. 6*: *"The atonement of Christ is not a mere skillful way to have our sins pardoned; it is a divine remedy for the cure of transgression and the restoration of spiritual health. It is the Heaven-ordained means by which the righteousness of Christ may be not only upon us, but in our hearts and characters"* (p. 1074).

I believe these comments, but more importantly, the previous Bible verses we looked at, are sufficient evidence to prove that a healing model is used throughout Scripture. As I stated earlier, the legal model has its purpose, but that purpose is limited.

On the other hand, it has been my experience that once a person is introduced to the healing model, a whole new world of understanding begins to open up for them. The grace of God and His marvelous plan of salvation to restore man to the image of God, for which he was first created, are brought clearly to view.

Not only that, but we are introduced to a new and enlightening picture of God, a God in whom there is nothing to fear, ever! We begin to see and understand more fully His perfect love that *"casteth out fear"* (1 John 4:18). And, just as a physician does not punish or destroy his patients, we see a God who does not arbitrarily punish or destroy but a God whose great desire is in healing and saving sinners.

In this model, we learn that the thing we must fear most is not God, but rather clinging to our sinful feelings of pride and self-sufficiency and refusing to come and co-operate with the Great Physician that He may heal us.

Now I will list the major points in this model. And just as we did with the legal model, in the next chapter, we will thoroughly examine each point.

First Point—God, the Almighty Creator who created all things in heaven and earth, created mankind in His own image. God loved the world and provided for all that was needed for its peace and happiness. However, God has a cruel and powerful enemy, Satan, who deceived the first humans and infected them with a rebellious spirit of mind and heart which resulted in the behavior we call sin.

Second Point—Sin is an inherited infection that produces hurtful symptoms like lying, stealing, false witness, murder, and eventually results in the death of its victim. The very first human couple was infected in the Garden of Eden. Since then, this disease has been passed from generation to generation. All human beings in this world are born infected with this rebellious spirit through no choice of their own.

Third Point—The root of this infection is in the mind. Because of that, it could be likened to a type of insanity. The suffering caused by this infectious insanity has caused untold suffering for the human race and its Creator. Man finds himself powerless to cure or to reverse the deadly effects of this disease.

Fourth Point—God, being able to see the end from the beginning, has planned for this emergency. The One who created the heavens and earth from nothing can create in human beings a new heart and right spirit. He is the Great Physician who can heal all our diseases and afflictions, physical or spiritual.

Fifth Point—In order for God to heal those afflicted with this terrible disease, there are certain things that must take place. The victim must be willing to come to Him, trusting that He knows what to do and is able to heal or save them. This is conversion, justification, or being "set right."

Sixth Point—Once a person has committed to cooperating with the Great Physician, they find that healing begins to take place immediately. Though they are not made completely well at once, as they continue to do their best to trust and follow Him, they get better and better. At last when the Lord returns, they find themselves completely well and in the very presence of God to live eternally. This is sanctification or being "kept right."

Seventh Point—Those who refuse to come to the Great Physician or who do not trust Him enough to carefully follow His prescribed treatments will eventually die. Not only the death of sleep to which all the human race is subject, but ultimately the second death. However, God does not stand as the executioner, but He leaves individuals to reap the consequences of their choices. They will then die the awful second death, as the Bible says, *"sin, when it is finished, bringeth forth death"* (James 1:15).

The heavenly Father, who has *"loved thee with an everlasting love"* (Jeremiah 31:3), will, just as a human parent, be terribly brokenhearted at the loss of His wayward children. He will weep over them as Jesus wept over Jerusalem long ago, but there is nothing more He can do. They are incurable. But in the end, the universe will be rid of the suffering, disease, pain, and death caused by sin, and those who have been redeemed, saved, and healed of the awful disease of sin will live eternally free.

These are the basic points of the healing model. This model, rather than being pre-occupied with forgiveness as the legal model, is focused on healing, restoration, and a final overcoming of sin and therefore the consequences of it.

I understand some may be alarmed by what I have presented here. Some, because of traditional beliefs, will, as the disciples who walked with Jesus and found some of His teachings hard to accept, find this hard to accept. It may seem so wrong, so different from what they have always heard that they will want to discard this book and its ideas.

I hope not, but in case you may think this model unworthy of consideration, before you dismiss it, please remember the words of King Solomon: *"He that answereth a matter before he heareth it, it is folly and shame unto him"* (Proverbs 18:13).

Before you answer this matter that I have raised, please take the time to read the next chapter as we take each point and consider the evidence provided for this model.

Chapter Seven

UNDERSTANDING THE HEALING MODEL

"But unto you that fear my name shall the Sun of righteousness arise with healing in his wings; and ye shall go forth, and grow up as calves of the stall" (Malachi 4:2).

In the previous chapter, we listed seven basic points of the healing model of the plan of salvation. In this chapter, we will examine those points and, at the same time, attempt to provide further evidence to support and better understand this model.

First Point

God, the Almighty Creator who created all things in heaven and earth, created mankind in His own image. God loved the world and provided for all that was needed for its peace and happiness. However, God has a cruel and powerful enemy, Satan, who deceived the first humans and infected them with a rebellious spirit of mind and heart which *resulted in the* behavior we call sin.

In the book of Genesis, we find the story of the creation of the earth and the tragic fall of our first parents, Adam and Eve. God created them as fully-grown, mature humans. He created every cell and organ in their bodies. God placed within their hearts and minds His law of unselfish love.

At the same time, He created them with free will and gave them the power to think, reason, learn, and make choices. He created them with the ability to procreate, to have children of their own. God told them to be fruitful and multiply and fill the earth. In the beginning, they were in complete harmony with God and the Holy angels. Every day, God came in person to the Garden and walked with them in the cool of the evening.

One fateful day, Eve found herself near the Tree of the Knowledge of Good and Evil, which God had warned them not to eat of. There at the tree, she heard the voice of a serpent speaking to her:

> "Yea, hath God said, Ye shall not eat of every tree of the garden?" To which Eve replied, "We may eat of the fruit of the trees of the garden: But of the fruit of the tree which is in the midst of the garden, God hath said, Ye shall not eat of it, neither shall ye touch it, lest ye die." To which the serpent made this bold rebuttal: "Ye shall not surely die: For God doth know that in the day ye eat thereof, then your eyes shall be opened, and ye shall be as gods, knowing good and evil" (Genesis 3:1-5).

Eve had listened to God. She was clear on what He had warned them of; she repeated it almost word for word. But now, as she listens to the serpent, she begins to give serious thought to what he is saying to her. Satan, speaking through the serpent, is basically saying that God has lied, that He can't be trusted, and to defy or to rebel against what God has said (the definition of sin) will not result in their death. Instead, Satan claims that it will enlighten them and give them even more wisdom. Then, *"knowing good and evil,"* knowing right from wrong themselves, they will be like God and won't need Him to tell them what to do.

I would venture a guess that Satan said to Eve something like this: "Death is something God is trying to frighten you with. There is no such thing as death! We are all immortal! Have you ever seen death? Have you ever heard of anyone dying? No, and no one else has either. God is just trying to frighten you so that you will remain a slave to His wishes."

In his twisted mind, Satan may have felt he was actually telling the truth, because up to that time, there had been no death in the entire universe. Here is where I believe Eve saw an excuse to doubt God's word. There was nothing God could point to and say, "This is what death is." There was no hard evidence. The more Eve thought about it, the more she became convinced that maybe the serpent was right.

Finally, her mind is made up—she sees no danger, only the possibility of exalting herself—and she eats of the forbidden tree. We all know the story.

After Eve eats, she gives some to Adam and he eats. They didn't notice anything at first, but later, when God came to visit them in the cool of the evening, they were afraid of Him. They had never been afraid before. They also suddenly realized they were "naked," that is, they felt exposed, and for the first time in their lives, they felt guilt.

When God asked them about it, they began to shift the blame for their actions. Adam blamed Eve; Eve blamed the serpent. Now it is evident that they are radically changed. They are experiencing feelings and demonstrating attitudes they have never had before.

When Adam and Eve made the decision to eat of the Tree of the Knowledge of Good and Evil, it was more than simply doing something God told them not to do. A radical change took place within their hearts and minds, and they were never the same.

Second Point

Sin is an inherited infection that produces hurtful symptoms like lying, stealing, false witness, murder, and eventually results in the death of its victim. The very first human couple was infected in the Garden of Eden. Since then, this disease has been passed from generation to generation. All human beings in this world are born infected with this rebellious spirit through no choice of their own.

Note the following comment from a book titled *God's Amazing Grace*:

> "Man was originally endowed with noble powers and a well-balanced mind. He was perfect in his being, and in harmony with God. His thoughts were pure, his aims holy. But through disobedience, his powers were perverted, and selfishness took the place of love. His nature became so weakened through transgression that it was impossible for him, in his own strength, to resist the power of evil. He was made captive by Satan, and would have remained so forever had not God specially interposed. It was the tempter's purpose to thwart the divine plan in man's creation, and fill the earth with woe and desolation" (p. 313).

"Selfishness took the place of love." What a tragedy! All one has to do is look at the history of mankind to see the horrible effect that this fact has had on the world since that time. Today, each one of us has suffered in many ways because of the great evil of selfishness. Selfishness is the root of all sin. Things like envy, jealously, hate, cheating, lying, stealing, adultery, murder, and any other harmful, hurtful behavior is simply the outward manifestation of the inner sickness of selfishness. It is this self-centered tendency that causes us to rebel against God.

An inspired writer looking upon the judgment scene wrote, *"Another book was opened, wherein were recorded the sins of those who profess the truth. Under the general heading of selfishness came every other sin"* (*The Faith I Live By*, p. 214).

The Bible says in Romans 5:12: *"Wherefore, as by one man sin entered into the world, and death by sin; and so death passed upon all men, for that all have sinned."* In other words, we are all born with that selfish-sinful nature inherited from Adam and Eve. That nature (human nature), if allowed to take its natural course, results in ruin and death.

Because selfishness is harmful and destructive and had taken such deep root in the nature of mankind, God drove Adam and Eve out of the Garden of Eden. No longer having access to the Tree of Life, they would eventually die. When God told them that they would die if they ate of the Tree of the Knowledge of Good and Evil, it was not a threat, as if He would have to execute them for disobedience to His command. Rather than a threat, it was a warning; a warning that if they chose to go against what He knew was best for them, they were actually cutting themselves off from the source of life, and they would die as the consequence. The fruit was like a deadly poison to them.

There is a lesson in this for us. If we, in our pride and self-centeredness, disregard God's Word, feeling that we are self sufficient and that we can determine for ourselves what is right and wrong—that we can go on our merry way without God—then we too are cutting ourselves off from the "Tree of Life," and we will die.

Let me stress once again, in the healing model, death is seen as the natural consequence of rebellion against God in that we cut ourselves off from the only source of life; we unplug our own life support system if you will. Whereas, in the legal model, we are executed for disobedience at God's direction as He orders that the sinner be cast into the lake of fire.

But the Bible is very clear on this; it plainly states: *"But every man is tempted, when he is drawn away of his own lust [desire and selfishness], and enticed. Then when lust hath conceived, it bringeth forth sin: and sin, when it is finished, bringeth forth death"* (James 1:14, 15), and, *"For the wages of sin is death"* (Romans 6:23).

Third Point

The root of this infection is in the mind. Because *of that*, it could be likened to a type of insanity. The suffering caused by this infectious insanity has caused untold suffering for the human race and its Creator. Man finds himself powerless to cure or to reverse the deadly effects of this disease.

The "heart" is mentioned some 850 times in the KJV Bible. The ancients believed that the organ called the heart is where man did his thinking. Today we know better. We know the heart is the organ that pumps blood throughout our bodies and that man's thinking is done in the head, in his brain. Understanding this, when we read about the heart in the Bible, we know that it is usually referring to a person's thoughts, beliefs, desires, and all those things that are developed in the mind.

Let's look at some examples:

- *"And GOD saw that the wickedness of man was great in the earth, and that every imagination of the thoughts of his heart [mind] was only evil continually"* (Genesis 6:5).

- *"And thou say in thine heart [mind], My power and the might of mine hand hath gotten me this wealth"* (Deuteronomy 8:17).

- *"The fool hath said in his heart [mind], There is no God. They are corrupt, they have done abominable works, there is none that doeth good"* (Psalms 14:1).

- *"Bow down thine ear, and hear the words of the wise, and apply thine heart [mind] unto my knowledge"* (Proverbs 22:17).

- *"For out of the heart [mind] proceed evil thoughts, murders, adulteries, fornications, thefts, false witness, blasphemies"* (Matthew 15:19).

The mind is the "control center" of our entire being. Within our minds are developed those things that make up our distinctive characters. Someone once said, "The mind is like a computer: garbage in, garbage out." That statement is probably truer than we would like to think.

Because of the "garbage" that most humans feed into their minds, the human race is on a dangerous path.

As we look back at the history of mankind, we can see that this is true. Many of the practices, attitudes, and lifestyles people enjoy are in reality destructive in the end. Yet, knowing that, they continue to cling to it, refusing to give it up—this is insanity!

How about you, dear reader? Is there something in your life that has proven to be hurtful to you or others, maybe even your family, yet you will not give it up? In Isaiah 1:5, the Bible says, *"The whole head is sick."* Aren't we all *"touched in the head"* to some extent, refusing to give up some cherished thing that is destroying us? It is insane, yet many of us do it!

Commenting on Isaiah 1:5, one author wrote, *"The whole head is sick, and the whole heart faint, and yet the sinner will brace himself in pride, and set up his will against the will of God. Though Christ is working upon human hearts, men utterly annul the work the Lord would do"* (*Review and Herald*, April 11, 1893).

Many self-help books have been written on the countless ways that mankind has developed in his attempt to rid himself of his self-destructive behavior. After thousands of years, it is painfully clear that mankind is not capable of healing himself of this deeply rooted problem.

This is not only a problem for mankind but for the Creator as well. In Isaiah 63:8, 9, the Bible says, *"So he was their Saviour. In all their affliction he was afflicted, and the angel of his presence saved them: in his love and in his pity he redeemed them; and he bare them, and carried them all the days of old."*

God cares deeply for His children. Just as a parent suffers when his child is stricken with a horrible disease and can find no rest or peace as long as his child suffers, so our heavenly Father suffers with us. In all our afflictions, He is afflicted! God will find no rest or peace until this nightmare of sin that sickens, maims, and destroys

His children is over. When we go to God for forgiveness we should remember this: sin is not simply breaking God's law and making Him angry, but it is breaking His heart and making Him hurt!

The healing model, seeing sin as insanity, helps us understand the words Christ uttered as He was being crucified. *"Father, forgive them; for they know not what they do"* (Luke 23:34). I want to emphasize that Christ's prayer was for those who were doing horrible things to Him. This is the perfect demonstration of unselfish love, of hating the sin but loving the sinner.

I use the following illustration to help us understand how this principle applies to the Christian. When parents have a child who is suffering from a serious mental disorder, the child may behave badly, even in hurtful ways. But, because the parents love their child unselfishly and know the child does not know what he is doing, they do not get angry with the child or punish him. Rather, they are patient with him and do all they can to help him.

I believe God sees us this way. He knows we are sin-sick, suffering from a serious mental disorder. As Jesus said, we don't know what we are doing, and He does not punish us but longs to help us. Read Psalms 103:10-14 again.

> "He hath not dealt with us after our sins; nor rewarded us according to our iniquities. For as the heaven is high above the earth, so great is his mercy toward them that fear him. As far as the east is from the west, so far hath he removed our transgressions from us. Like as a father pitieth his children, so the LORD pitieth them that fear him. For he knoweth our frame; he remembereth that we are dust."

This should help us to understand what it means to hate the sin, but love the sinner. When we see another person behaving badly, instead of looking at them as a great sinner, we should remember that they are behaving that way because they have a serious mental disorder.

They are not criminals; they are sick. They don't really know what they are doing. And the worse a person is behaving, the sicker they are, and the sicker they are, the more they need our help, not our condemnation!

We all have this sickness, but some are in worse condition than others. This is why the Bible says that we should comfort one another, help one another, and encourage one another, instead of judging and criticizing one another.

Fourth Point

God, being able to see the end from the beginning, has planned for this emergency. The One who created the heavens and earth from nothing can create in human beings a new heart and right spirit. He is the Great Physician who can heal all our diseases and afflictions, physical or spiritual.

"Blessed be the God and Father of our Lord Jesus Christ, who hath blessed us with all spiritual blessings in heavenly places in Christ: According as he hath chosen us in him before the foundation of the world, that we should be holy and without blame before him in love" (Ephesians 1:3, 4).

From this text, it is clear that God had planned before the creation of the world a way to rescue those, who through no fault of their own, are born in this sin infested world.

After his great sin, David prayed this prayer as recorded in Psalms 51:9, 10: *"Hide thy face from my sins, and blot out all mine iniquities. Create in me a clean heart, O God; and renew a right spirit within me."* The Lord God, being the Creator of all things, is certainly able to create in us a clean heart and repair any damage done to our hearts or minds.

Once we realize that we are sin-sick and that we cannot heal ourselves, we must find a good physician, one who is qualified to administer the remedy that will bring the healing we need. The Bible says:

> "Be it known unto you all, and to all the people of Israel, that by the name of Jesus Christ of Nazareth, whom ye crucified, whom God raised from the dead, even by him doth this man stand here before you whole. This is the stone which was set at nought of you builders, which is become the head of the corner. Neither is there salvation [healing] in any other: for there is none other name under heaven given among men, whereby we must be saved [sozo–healed]" (Acts 4:10-12).

The Bible also says, *"Bless the LORD, O my soul, and forget not all his benefits: Who forgiveth all thine iniquities; who healeth all thy diseases; Who redeemeth thy life from destruction; who crowneth thee with lovingkindness and tender mercies"* (Psalms 103:2-4). Jesus Christ is the Great Physician who can heal all our diseases!

Fifth Point

In order for God to heal those afflicted with this terrible disease, there are certain things that must take place. The victim must be willing to come to Him, trusting that He knows what to do and is able to heal or save them. This is conversion, justification, or being "set right."

To help illustrate this point, I will use the example of the alcoholic. Medical science has learned that many alcoholics are born with great potential for the disease of alcoholism in their genes or DNA. For those in this condition, it is almost impossible for them to control their drinking once they start. They are held captive to their addiction. Yet many alcoholics are in denial and will not face the fact that they have a problem.

In order for them to have any hope of recovery, they must first acknowledge or "confess" that they have a problem. Once they admit they have a problem, they can begin to take steps to correct it.

Those who look within themselves for the power to overcome soon realize they are powerless to overcome their addiction. It is at this point, they must begin to seek help from other sources. Those who find the help they need and faithfully follow the prescribed program, although they still have the genes within their bodies and will as long as they live, can overcome their addiction and live without alcohol. The alcoholic does not have to drink; they can overcome.

The sinner, just as the alcoholic, is born with sin in his DNA, and just as with the alcoholic, it is impossible for him in his own strength to control his behavior. Man is held captive to his selfish, sinful nature. Just as with the alcoholic, many people are in denial as to their sinful condition.

Like Adam and Eve, they try to put the blame on someone else for their misdeeds. But to have any hope of recovery, they must first acknowledge and confess that they have a serious problem. This is why the Apostle John wrote: *"If we confess our sins, he is faithful and just to forgive us our sins, and to cleanse us from all unrighteousness"* (1 John 1:9).

In the legal model, many feel they must remember every sin they have ever committed and confess them one by one. That can be frightening, because if they forget one, they're in trouble, believing every single one must be named and repented of. Otherwise, it remains on the books as being not forgiven. What a burden! That's the legal model way of thinking. That way of thinking makes God look demanding and harsh, but God knows our weaknesses, He knows we couldn't possibly remember every little sin we have ever committed!

On the other hand, in the healing model, all we need to confess is that we are sinners in need of help and healing; in need of forgiveness and cleansing from all our unrighteousness, collectively. Recognizing our condition and acknowledging it through confession is the first step in our recovery. Just as the alcoholic, as long as we live in this corrupt body, we will have the potential to sin. That's what John was referring to when he said, *"If we say that we have no sin, we deceive ourselves, and the truth is not in us"* (1 John 1:8).

In other words, no matter how much we have grown spiritually, if we say we don't have the potential to sin, we are in denial. We are saying we are not sick, we are no longer infected. But all of us, saved or lost, have the potential to sin, because we are all sinners by nature. We are living in corrupt bodies and we will be until Jesus comes. Then, *"In a moment, in the twinkling of an eye, at the last trump: for the trumpet shall sound, and the dead shall be raised incorruptible, and we shall be changed. For this corruptible must put on incorruption, and this mortal must put on immortality."* (1 Corinthians 15:52-53).

The major difference between the saved and the lost is that the saved are in the recovery process and the lost are not—they remain in denial or are working hard attempting to heal themselves! Salvation is not an event. It is a process. As long as we are in the recovery process, we can have the wonderful assurance of salvation in the end.

Again, using the alcoholic metaphor, just because we have the potential to sin because it's in our DNA or genetic makeup doesn't mean that we have to sin, no more than an alcoholic has to drink. According to the Bible, we can overcome, but in order for us to overcome, we need help. We cannot do it in our own strength. We need the Great Physician!

According to the Word of God, He *"is able to keep you from falling, and to present you faultless before the presence of his glory with exceeding joy"* (Jude 1:24). I believe He can do what He says, how about you?

If we go to a physician with a medical problem, he may say we need to take some medication or do some exercise or maybe even have surgery. If we refuse, we will not recover.

In the same way, once we acknowledge our condition and come to the Great Physician for treatment, we must have enough trust or faith in Him to be willing to do the things He prescribes. If we are unwilling to do those things He says are needed, we will not get well; we will not be saved or healed! This is "saving faith," trusting God enough to do those things He says we should do.

You may remember the words of Christ to the rich young ruler: *"If thou wilt enter into life, keep the commandments"* (Matthew 19:17). I found it interesting that the word "commandment" is translated from the Greek word "entole," and it can be defined as an "authoritative prescription." In other words, something prescribed by one who is an expert authority. That expert authority can be none other than God when it comes to salvation (healing of the sin-sick soul).

By pointing this out, I am not advocating salvation by works here. Rather, in this model, the works is that which comes as a natural result or fruit of the relationship with and faith in the Great Physician. Ephesians 2:8-10 says it very clearly: *"For by grace are ye saved through faith; and that not of yourselves: it is the gift of God: Not of works, lest any man should boast. For we are his workmanship, created in Christ Jesus unto good works, which God hath before ordained that we should walk in them."*

Did you notice the words *"created in Christ Jesus unto good works"*? Not by good works or with good works but unto or for good works! This is made clear in the book *Steps To Christ*:

> "We do not earn salvation by our obedience; for salvation is the free gift of God, to be received by faith. But obedience is the fruit of faith. "Ye know that He was manifested to take away our sins; and in Him is no sin. Whosoever abideth in Him sinneth not: whosoever sinneth hath not seen Him, neither known Him." 1 John 3:5, 6. Here is the true test. If we abide in Christ, if the love of God dwells in us, our feelings, our thoughts, our purposes, our actions, will be in harmony with the will

of God as expressed in the precepts of His holy law"
(p. 59).

That so-called faith in Christ that professes to release
men from the obligation of obedience to God is not faith
but presumption. *"By grace are ye saved through faith,"*
but *"faith, if it hath not works, is dead"* (Ephesians 2:8
and James 2:17).

Salvation is not about *what we do* as much as it is
about *what we are!* We are all born defective. You might
have heard the old saying, *"God loves you just as you are,
but He doesn't want you to stay that way."* We do need forgiveness because of guilt, but even more, we need to *be
changed* if we are going to be safe to save.

Remember the story of Isaiah and King Manasseh?
We will never get into heaven clinging to our sin! We must
change, and change can be, and usually is, a difficult and
sometimes painful process.

Theologians have come up with many theories of salvation to convince people that they can be saved without
going through the painful process of change or that they
can be saved without overcoming those old comfortable
sinful habits. That is a subtle and deadly deception.

Look at the following text from Galatians and the
promises from the book of Revelation:

- *"Be not deceived; God is not mocked: for whatsoever a
man soweth, that shall he also reap. For he that soweth
to his flesh shall of the flesh reap corruption; but he
that soweth to the Spirit shall of the Spirit reap life
everlasting"* (Galatians 6:7, 8).

- *"To him that overcometh will I give to eat of the tree of
life"* (Revelation 2:7).

- *"He that overcometh shall not be hurt of the second
death"* (Revelation 2:11).

- *"He that overcometh, the same shall be clothed in white raiment; and I will not blot out his name out of the book of life"* (Revelation 3:5).

We cannot declare, "Jesus has done it all," and then sit back and coast into heaven. We must, just as the Apostle Paul taught us, *"work out your salvation with fear and trembling"* (Philippians 2:12) and *"fight the good fight of faith"* (1 Timothy 6:12), if we are to enter into the gates of the beloved city of God.

This does not mean working our way into God's good graces. But we must find the time to spend with God that He can do His work in us. Finding time for this in our busy lives may be our greatest fight.

Jesus made the steps we need to take very clear as recorded in Luke 6:46-48:

> "And why call ye me, Lord, Lord, and do not the things which I say? Whosoever cometh to me, and heareth my sayings, and doeth them, I will shew you to whom he is like: He is like a man which built an house, and digged deep, and laid the foundation on a rock: and when the flood arose, the stream beat vehemently upon that house, and could not shake it: for it was founded upon a rock. But he that heareth, and doeth not, is like a man that without a foundation built an house upon the earth; against which the stream did beat vehemently, and immediately it fell; and the ruin of that house was great".

In this passage, Jesus points out the three important steps to overcoming sin as we have outlined in the healing model: (1) come to Me, (2) hear My sayings, and (3) do them.

Sixth Point

Once a person has committed to cooperating with the Great Physician, they find that healing begins to take place immediately. Though they are not made completely well at once, as they continue to do their best to trust and follow Him, they get better and better. At last when the Lord returns, they find themselves completely well and in the very presence of God to live eternally. This is sanctification or being "kept right."

Jesus said very clearly in John 15:4-6, "*Abide in me, and I in you. As the branch cannot bear fruit of itself, except it abide in the vine; no more can ye, except ye abide in me. I am the vine, ye are the branches: He that abideth in me, and I in him, the same bringeth forth much fruit: for without me ye can do nothing. If a man abide not in me, he is cast forth as a branch, and is withered; and men gather them, and cast them into the fire, and they are burned.*"

Again, with the healing model, if I am faithful to keep my appointments with the physician in charge of my case and am careful to follow his counsel, I will get well.

In the same way, a believer should be careful to keep his appointments with the Great Physician, with the most important appointment being the Sabbath. Then there are those daily appointments too, the quiet times of devotion that are needed to help keep us spiritually healthy day by day. The recovering believer is careful to follow the prescribed directions of the Great Physician, following closely all the counsel found in His Word. This is sanctification, or to use the simpler term, "being kept right."

In the healing model, a person is cooperating with the Great Physician so that the cancer of sin goes into remission. Then, at the close of the investigative judgment, Christ makes an announcement: "*He that is unjust, let him be unjust still: and he which is filthy, let him be filthy still: and he that is righteous, let him be righteous still: and he that is holy, let him be holy still. And, behold, I come quick-*

ly; and my reward is with me, to give every man according as his work shall be" (Revelation 22:11, 12).

This is not a judge declaring who is legally pardoned or who is condemned as in the legal model; rather, in the healing model, this is the Great Physician's diagnosis of who is healed and safe to allow entrance into the Kingdom of God.

Seventh Point

Those who refuse to come to the Great Physician or who do not trust Him enough to carefully follow His prescribed treatments will eventually die. Not only the death of sleep to which all the human race is subject, but ultimately the second death. However, God does not stand as the executioner, but He leaves individuals to reap the consequences of their choices. They will then die the awful second death, as the Bible says *"sin when it is finished, bringeth forth death"* (James 1:15).

The heavenly Father who has *"loved thee with an everlasting love"* (Jeremiah 31:3), will, just as a human parent, be terribly brokenhearted at the loss of His wayward children. He will weep over them as Jesus wept over Jerusalem long ago, but there is nothing more He can do. They are incurable. But in the end, the universe will be rid of the suffering, disease, pain, and death caused by sin, and those who have been redeemed, saved, and healed of the awful disease of sin will live eternally free.

Let me state once more, the healing model, rather than being pre-occupied with forgiveness, is focused on healing, restoration, the final overcoming of sin, and therefore, the consequences of it.

The physician is an authority in healing and knows what to prescribe for the sick patient to make him well, but a doctor cannot help patients who do not trust him enough to do the things he says.

A story is told of a man who had smoked two packs of cigarettes a day for 30 years. His doctor, who was also a close friend, pleaded with him and did everything he could think of to get him to quit smoking, but to no avail. His smoker friend was unwilling to go through the pain of change, and now his lungs are completely destroyed by incurable lung cancer. The doctor is broken hearted. He will forgive his friend for smoking all those cigarettes, but there is nothing more he can do but sadly watch him die.

Doctors may love their sick patients. They may forgive them for not taking their medicine or following their instructions, but the patient will not get well, because love and forgiveness will not heal the damage done by the continued damaging behavior.

Does a doctor punish his patients for being sick or not taking their medicine? Of course not! Oh sure, some of the treatments he must administer may be painful, but they are not designed to punish but to bring healing as a result. In the same way, God does not punish us for our sin-sick behavior. But He does allow the consequences of sin many times to bring pain to us so that we will come to our senses and turn from our sin and turn to Him for help. He helps us stop the sin so recovery can begin.

Do doctors kill their dying patients? Again, of course not. They do everything they can to save them. Then what about the Great Physician? What about God? Would He do any less? Does God kill His dying children? Of course not! It is sin that kills. As one author wrote, *"As leprosy was sure death if permitted to take its natural course, so the leprosy of sin will destroy the sinner unless they received the healing of the grace of God"* (*Signs of the Times*, March 14, 1892).

God, our gracious Father, rather than condemning us, is desperately trying to save us. Not so He won't have to punish us, but so that the leprosy of sin will not destroy us! *"For the wages of sin is death; but the gift of God is eternal life through Jesus Christ our Lord"* (Romans 6:23).

Bottom line: Sin is the source of death, and God is the source of life!

The following statement (in light of all the evidence available), found in the book *The Great Controversy*, adds more weight to the argument as to whether or not the wicked die at God's hand or as the natural consequence of sin.

> "God does not stand toward the sinner as an executioner of the sentence against transgression; but He leaves the rejecters of His mercy to themselves, to reap that which they have sown. Every ray of light rejected, every warning despised or unheeded, every passion indulged, every transgression of the law of God, is a seed sown, which yields its unfailing harvest" (p. 36).

Leaving *"the rejecters of His mercy to themselves to reap that which they have sown"* or to reap the consequences of their choices is a solid biblical principle. Again, *"Do not be deceived, God is not mocked; for whatsoever a man soweth, that shall he will also reap. For he that soweth to his flesh shall of the flesh reap corruption; but he that soweth to the Spirit shall of the Spirit reap everlasting life"* (Galatians 6:7, 8).

When this view is presented, the question always comes up: But what about God's wrath? The wrath of God is misunderstood by most people to be like man's wrath, but God says, *"My ways [are] higher than your ways"* (Isaiah 55:9). Again, we must be careful that we do not make God in our image. He is not like us! If we let the Bible interpret itself, we will find the true understanding of God's wrath.

Note the following biblical example of how God's wrath works: *"Then my anger shall be kindled against them in that day, and I will forsake them, and I will hide my face from them, and they shall be devoured, and many evils and troubles shall befall them; so that they will say in that day. Are not these evils come upon us, because our God is not among us?"* (Deuteronomy 31:17)

Why are evils and troubles befalling them? God is not among them. God has given them up to the consequences of their own choice to reject Him and follow man's counsel.

We see this again in another passage: *"But my people would not hearken to my voice; and Israel would none of me. So I gave them up unto their own hearts' lust: and they walked in their own counsels"* (Psalms 81:11, 12).

In the New Testament, Paul describes in the book of Romans this same understanding of God's wrath. He gives those up who persist in going their own way, disregarding His instruction and guidance for their good.

"For the wrath of God is revealed from heaven against all ungodliness and unrighteousness of men, who hold the truth in unrighteousness; Because that which may be known of God is manifest in them; for God hath shewed it unto them. For the invisible things of him from the creation of the world are clearly seen, being understood by the things that are made, even his eternal power and Godhead; so that they are without excuse:

Because that, when they knew God, they glorified him not as God, neither were thankful; but became vain in their imaginations, and their foolish heart was darkened. Professing themselves to be wise, they became fools, and changed the glory of the uncorruptible God into an image made like to corruptible man, and to birds, and fourfooted beasts, and creeping things.

Wherefore God also gave them up to uncleanness through the lusts of their own hearts....Who changed the truth of God into a lie, and worshipped and served the creature more than the Creator, who is blessed for ever. Amen.

For this cause God gave them up unto vile affections....And even as they did not like to retain God in their knowledge, God gave them over [The Greek is the same as the other verse, "gave them up"] to a reprobate mind" (Romans 1:18-28).

Again, God's wrath is not like man's anger—getting mad and getting even. God's wrath is God giving up those who insist on going their own destructive way and allowing them to suffer the consequences. God does not impose an external punishment upon them. He does not beat them up or burn them up. But, after doing all He can to reach them, He will simply, yet sadly, give them up to do what they want, and they will reap the unpleasant results God has been trying to warn them against and keep them from.

When people, in this way, persistently cut themselves off from the source of life and good, what will happen to them? They will suffer and eventually die.

All one has to do to understand how the wicked die is to go to the cross. Jesus died that death experiencing the "wrath of God." If the wrath of God that punishes the sinner is being given up, we should have a text that says Jesus was given up, and we do in the book of Romans.

- *"Now it was not written for his sake alone, that it was imputed to him; but also for us, to whom it shall be imputed, if we believe on him who raised up Jesus our Lord from the dead, who was delivered for our offenses, and was raised again for our justification"* (Romans 4:23-25).

- *"What then shall we say to these things? If God be for us, who can be against us? He that spared not his own Son, but delivered him up for us all, how shall he not with him also freely give us all things?"* (Romans 8:31, 32).

In both of these texts, the word translated *"delivered up"* and *"delivered Him up"* is the same Greek word we just read in Romans chapter one, where it is translated *"given up."* Sensing that He had been "given up" by God is what prompted the cry from the lips of Jesus: *"My God, my God, why hast thou forsaken me?"* (Matthew 27:46). In other words, *"Why have you given me up?"*

Christ, having been *"made...sin for us"* (2 Corinthians 5:21), suffered the ultimate consequences of sin on the cross. He experienced what the lost will experience at the end of time as they *"drink of the cup of the wrath of God."* That is, as they experience the painful realization that they have cut themselves off from God, the only source of life, and instead of freedom and life eternal, their portion is eternal death. Then, the overwhelming, burning emotional pain of despair, guilt, and self-condemnation will consume them.

"Therefore have I poured out mine indignation upon them; I have consumed them with the fire of my wrath: their own way have I recompensed upon their heads, saith the Lord GOD" (Ezekiel 22:31).

"Their own way have I recompensed upon their heads." God simply gives them up to experience the consequences of that which they have chosen. I believe the following sums up this idea.

"God destroys no man; but after a time the wicked are given up to the destruction they have wrought for themselves. When a man chooses his own way in the face of light and evidence, and refuses to be admonished, and to turn to the Lord with contrition of soul, the next message the Lord shall send will have less effect, for he allows his independent, self-willed spirit to control his judgment. He continues to cast the seed of resistance into his heart, and every time he repeats his act of resistance, refusing to turn from his own way to God's way, he bends his inclination in the way of disobedience, loves rebellion, and at last becomes callous, and the seed of unbelief ripens for the harvest" (*The Youth's Instructor*, November 30, 1893).

When the subject of God destroying the wicked comes up, someone always asks, "What about the flood? Doesn't that prove God destroys or kills?" Think about this. Did God destroy them or did He simply put them to sleep (put them in a spiritual "time out") until the resurrection?

Did not Jesus say as recorded in John 5:28, 29: *"Marvel not at this: for the hour is coming, in the which all that are in the graves shall hear his voice, and shall come forth; they that have done good, unto the resurrection of life; and they that have done evil, unto the resurrection of damnation."*?

All those He "destroyed" in the past He will make alive again; they are not dead but asleep. God is not a murderer, a killer, or an executioner! We will study the death of the wicked in detail in chapter ten of this book.

If God, as taught in the legal model, arbitrarily punishes the sinner, then we need pardon to avoid the punishment. But, if as in the healing model, sin is a sickness that produces suffering and death, then we need healing: we need the Great Physician!

We have nothing to fear from God regardless of who we are or what we have done. What we must fear is the selfish, rebellious heart that resists coming to God for the healing that only He can provide. Only He can give us peace, freedom, and eternal life. And those who will come to Him, He will by no means turn away.

There may still be questions as to the part forgiveness plays in this model. And what about God's justice? What role do these things play in the healing model? In the next two chapters, we will take a closer look at forgiveness and God's justice to better understand their role in God's plan.

The contrast between these two models can be clearly seen in the following table.

The Legal Model	The Healing Model
God is the Creator and as such has (arbitrarily) proclaimed His law by which man is to be governed.	God created the universe based on certain laws which are natural and immutable, love being the foundational law.
An arbitrary, external, predetermined penalty will be rendered upon those who disobey God's law.	Violators of God's law will suffer the natural consequence that results from violating God's good laws.
All humans are violators of the law; all are born guilty and condemned to punishment and ultimately death.	All humans are born infected with a rebellious, selfish nature which will eventually consume and destroy them.
Those who do not repent and turn from their sinful behavior will be cast alive into a lake of fire. To avoid that, man must be pardoned/forgiven.	To avoid destruction, man must be healed of his deadly infection, forgiveness being only a part of that process.
Since man cannot save himself, the innocent Son of God came and paid the penalty for the guilty so God could pardon him.	Since man cannot heal himself, God sent His Son that by His life and death man may be won back to faith in God for the healing of their deadly infection.
If a person accepts Christ as Savior, he is pardoned and will not be punished but granted eternal life. Those who reject Christ are cast into the lake of fire.	If man comes to God and cooperates with Him, he will be healed and live eternally. Those who refuse cut themselves off from the only source of life and will ultimately die from infection.
God is judge and executioner. He will have all sinners cast into the lake of fire.	God is the Great Physician and the only source of life. He alone can heal the sin-sick and restore life to the dying.

Chapter Eight

THE MEANING OF FORGIVENESS

"If we confess our sins, he is faithful and just to forgive us our sins, and to cleanse us from all unrighteousness" (1 John 1:9).

It is easy to understand the part forgiveness plays in the legal model, but where does forgiveness fit into the healing model? We will answer that in this chapter.

There have been many books and articles written and countless sermons preached on forgiveness. After much study on this subject, it seems to me there are two ways of understanding forgiveness. There is man's way and God's way. I will begin with man's way.

To do that, we begin with Webster's dictionary definition of the word "forgiveness:" (1) To grant pardon (in a legal sense), (2) To grant freedom from penalty; cease to demand penalty, and (3) To remit, as a debt.

There are basically two situations where someone may seek forgiveness from another: (1) When one has offended or hurt another or (2) When one is indebted to another.

The result of these situations is that some sort of penalty or payback is usually required. In order for the guilty or obligated party to avoid the penalty or payback, there must be forgiveness or pardon by the one offended or the one to whom the debt is owed.

Someone once said, *"forgiveness to the injured belongs."* In man's way of thinking, it is understood that the injured party has the exclusive right to grant or refuse forgiveness.

Some people choose to freely forgive, to remit the penalty, or to free from the debt owed. To these people, peace and love is the priority. Others will forgive only if the one who has offended them demonstrates true sorrow for what they have done and comes to them begging their mercy.

Still others choose not to forgive at all. They insist on "justice" (this topic will be discussed more fully in the next chapter). They cannot have peace until the offending party gets what's coming to them and the penalty or debt is paid in full! If that is not forthcoming as they feel it should be, these people choose to cling to their offended and embittered feelings and will not let them go.

There is a story about a man long ago who was bitten by a dog with rabies. Back in those days, they had no vaccine for rabies and to contract this disease was a death sentence. After his examination, the doctor told the man the horrifying news: "Get your affairs in order; it's just a matter of time. We will keep you as comfortable as we can, but there is no cure." The doctor then left the room.

The man picked up a piece of paper and started writing. The doctor momentarily re-entered the room and saw the patient writing on this paper. The doctor said, "Well, I see you are writing out your will."

"No," the man replied, "I'm not writing my will, I'm writing a list of names of all the people I'm going to bite before I die!"

In our world, clinging to feelings of animosity and bitterness against those who have offended us is seen as acceptable, even normal. The Christian believer, however, must ask, is this Christ-like? Is this God's way? We find the answer in the Bible, not the dictionary.

The original biblical Hebrew and Greek words translated "forgiveness," "forgiven," and "forgive," all have basically the same definition: (1) To send away or (2) To release; to let go.

Penalty or punishment is not mentioned in the definition. The reason for this may be, as we've discussed previously, according to Galatians 6:7, when there is an offense, there is automatically a penalty: *"Whatsoever a man soweth, that shall he also reap."*

This basic principle established by God has never failed, nor will it ever fail. It is a fact of life; every deed, every word, every gesture, and every action in life, on both the physical and spiritual plane, has a sure consequence.

Right actions result in good consequences. Wrong actions result in bad consequences in which somebody gets hurt.

For example: A man lies on the witness stand and because of that an innocent person is sent to prison. Years later, the man who lied repents and recants his testimony, and the innocent man is freed. If the person injured in this case forgives his false accuser, does that give him back all those years of suffering in prison? No. Or, if a man commits adultery and later feels remorse and asks to be forgiven by his wife and his wife graciously forgives him, does that make the hurt go away for his wife? No.

The damage done by actions that offend and hurt do not disappear when the offended party grants forgiveness. There are sure consequences to our actions and the only way to change the consequences is to change the actions! So, if forgiveness does not remit or heal the damage done to the offended party, what is the advantage? Why should the one who is offended forgive?

Let me answer that question with a question. When a person sincerely, from the heart, forgives the one who has offended them, does that act free him from feelings of animosity and bitterness within? Yes! If you don't believe it, try it!

Do you remember the biblical meaning of forgiveness? Basically, it means *to let go*. So, when a person chooses to forgive, to let go of the bitterness and animosity, who benefits most from the act of forgiveness? The one who is forgiven, or the one who forgives? To forgive, *to let go* of the anger, bitterness, and hatred has a healing effect on the inner person of the offended person—that's why God says to do it! And if we come to love like He does, it will come naturally.

That is why Jesus said, *"And when ye stand praying, forgive, if ye have ought against any: that your Father also which is in heaven may also forgive you your trespasses. But if ye do not forgive, neither will your Father in heaven forgive your trespasses"*(Mark 11:25, 26).

In other words, if we are holding feelings of contempt and bitterness for another and will not forgive (*let it go*), it becomes more hurtful to us than to them, and therefore, it becomes a sin in itself. And if we will not repent of that, what can God do? He is willing to let it go, but we are not willing to let it go. Clinging to an unforgiving attitude, holding within bitterness and hate for another, even if they deserve it, is like poison in your spirit, and it will eventually destroy you. Someone once said, *"He who chooses vengeance needs to dig two graves."* We have to let it go!

A friend of Clara Barton, founder of the American Red Cross, once reminded her of an especially cruel thing done to her years before. But Miss Barton seemed not to recall it. *"Don't you remember it?"* her friend asked. *"No,"* came the reply, *"I distinctly remember forgetting that."* She made a deliberate choice to let it go—the true meaning of forgiveness.

Now let's take a look at how God forgives. As we do, let's look again at the two following passages.

- *"These things hast thou done, and I kept silence; thou thoughtest that I was altogether such an one as thyself; but I will reprove thee, and set them in order before thine eyes"* (Psalms 50:21).

- *"For my thoughts are not your thoughts, neither are your ways my ways, saith the LORD. For as the heavens are higher than the earth, so are my ways higher than your ways, and my thoughts than your thoughts"* (Isaiah 55:8, 9).

Again, remember, God does not think like we do! This seems to be a difficult lesson for us to learn. We keep trying to make God in our image. We think He would react to certain situations like we would, but God says, no, I am not like you.

So, when we read a text like Psalms 7:11 that says, *"God is angry with the wicked every day,"* how are we to understand that? Does God hold bitterness, animosity, and anger in His heart like we do? Is He waiting on the sinner to come begging His forgiveness, and if he doesn't, there is "hell to pay"? I don't think so.

When the Bible speaks of God's anger, it is not like ours—*getting mad and getting even.* The word "anger" in the dictionary is defined as *"extreme or passionate displeasure,"* and it can mean *getting mad,* but, it can also mean the extreme, passionate heartbreak a parent feels when his child does something dreadfully wrong. The parent is not mad, but rather heartbroken, feeling both hurt and concern for the child.

In the same way, our heavenly Father is not *mad at us* but is passionately concerned for our wellbeing. Remember:

> "He hath not dealt with us after our sins; nor rewarded us according to our iniquities. For as the heaven is high above the earth, so great is his mercy toward them that fear him. As far as the east is from the west, so far hath he removed our transgressions from us. Like as a father pitieth his children, so the LORD pitieth them that fear him. For he knoweth our frame; he remembereth that we are dust" (Psalms 103:10-14).

There's a little story that may help you better understand our heavenly Father's forgiveness. A little boy sneaks into his parents' bedroom in the morning before they awaken. Going to where his father laid his pants the night before, he slips his little hand into the pocket and pulls out some change and quickly leaves.

His father, however, is not asleep; he had one eye open. He saw his son take the money. Now, the father won't go broke because he lost a few coins, but he feels terrible. Why? Because of what his son did. He is concerned about the consequences for the boy if he continues this kind of behavior. It is not about the money but about the relationship. The father is hurt.

Does he stop loving the boy? Does he think, "He is no longer my son until he makes this right? Until he comes and begs my forgiveness?" No, he loves the boy even more! The father feels *"passionate displeasure"* (Webster's definition of anger), but he is not mad at his son!

Later, the boy begins to feel sorry for what he has done. He goes to his father, hands him the money and says, *"Dad, I stole this from you. I'm sorry, will you forgive me?"* The father puts his hand on the boy's shoulder and says, *"Son, of course I forgive you."*

Does that mean that for the first time since the boy stole the money his father now extends forgiveness? Has his father been holding this against his son since that morning? No, the boy has been forgiven all along; his father never held it against him. But the son did not know that, and because of his feeling of guilt, he needed to know that his dad forgave him. So when he confessed, his dad said to his son, *"I forgive you."* (Original story told by Richard Nies in his book, *The Security of Salvation*.)

Those who have children of their own understand this. If their child were to get into serious trouble with the law or get addicted to drugs, if they love their child, they won't be angry; instead, they will be deeply troubled and concerned and will want to reach out to their child to help him/her. They want their child to come to them asking for their help, not begging forgiveness. The child, however, may come to feel the need to ask for their forgiveness.

So, in case you need to know that God will forgive you, 1 John 1:9 says, *"If we confess our sins, he is faithful and just to forgive us our sins."* Just like the child who has gotten into trouble, if we go to God and say, *"Father, I have done wrong, please forgive me,"* He will say, *"of course I forgive you."* The truth is that in reality He forgave us before we asked. As a matter of fact, just as the loving parent, He never held it against us in the first place!

The Bible stresses that *"His mercy is from everlasting to everlasting"* and that *"God never changes."* This means that God always, constantly, compassionately forgives—God *"lets it go."* The problem is we have been deceived and don't know that! Many are reluctant to come to God because they feel He is angry with them and that He might not forgive them. That's Satan's picture of God intended to discourage us. God wants us to know that we are forgiven. That's why Jesus cried from the cross, *"Father, forgive them"* even though no one asked, no one confessed, and no one repented!

The author of *The Desire of Ages* puts it this way: *"That prayer of Christ for His enemies embraced the world. It took in every sinner that had lived or should live, from the beginning of the world to the end of time. Upon all rests the guilt of crucifying the Son of God. To all, forgiveness is freely offered"* (p. 745).

Love and forgiveness was in God's heart before Christ died! That is His nature. That's one reason why He died, so we would know that. When we go to the cross and realize that in spite of our sin, God never has and never will feel bitter or resentful toward us, but only and always compassion and love for you and for me, we see Him with new eyes. It is this redeeming love that draws us to God.

When we realize the depth of this kind of love, we then understand that it is the *"goodness of God that leadeth thee to repentance"* (Romans 2:4). It transforms our heart and changes our mind about the way we live and about the way we see God! This is what it means to be *"redeemed by the blood of the Lamb."* This is the redeeming love we sing about.

To summarize the message of this chapter, God's forgiveness isn't a reward system where if you beg and plead enough God lets you off the hook. No, God has already forgiven us and what we call "being forgiven," is in reality, our coming to accept His forgiveness that has been there all along.

For you and me, for men and women, forgiveness is more about the healing it brings the one who is doing the forgiving than it is about the one who has caused harm. This understanding of forgiveness is a part of the healing model.

Remember, it is not God who condemns us but rather it is sin that condemns us. God's *forgiveness* will not *"remit the penalty;"* forgiveness does not stop the consequences of sin. However, if we let Him, God, by transforming our sinful nature, will help us stop the sin, and then there will be no painful consequences.

God's forgiveness is not for sale. God didn't say, *"I will forgive you if..."* You didn't change and then God forgave you; you realized God forgave you and then you changed.

Someone may object to this way of looking at God's forgiveness as being too soft, insisting that God is a God of justice. I am sure you have heard many people say, "Yes, God is loving, but He is also just." What about God's justice? Is it comparable to our legal court system of justice? We will examine that in the next chapter.

Chapter Nine

GOD'S JUSTICE

"Dearly beloved, avenge not yourselves, but rather give place unto wrath: for it is written, Vengeance is mine; I will repay, saith the Lord. Therefore if thine enemy hunger, feed him; if he thirst, give him drink: for in so doing thou shalt heap coals of fire on his head" (Romans 12:19).

Among preachers today, God's grace and mercy are given a lot of emphasis. But have you noticed that we don't hear any "fire and brimstone" sermons anymore? I believe the reason is not so much that hell is an unpopular topic people don't want to hear any more, but that most preachers find it difficult to explain it in a way that makes sense.

How can God, whom the Bible says is love and who never changes, turn and punish those who reject His love and offers of mercy by casting them into a lake of fire where they will, as some believe, slowly and agonizingly burn forever, or at best, slowly burn to death? In an attempt to reconcile this confusing contradiction, it is said, *"God is not only loving; He is just!"*

But before we let it go at that, I would like to ask the question: What does that mean? What is God's justice? Are we to liken it to man's justice? Let's take a closer look.

In the King James Version Bible, the English word *"justice"* is used only in the Old Testament and is translated from a Hebrew word that simply means *"rightness."*

The English word *"justice"* is not in the New Testament at all; instead, we find in its place the word *"just"* translated from a Greek word which has the same meaning as the Hebrew, *"righteous or rightness."* Both of these words meaning *"rightness,"* which in some places is correctly translated *"right"* or *"righteous"* but in other places *"just"* or *"justice,"* which give them legal overtones.

The problem is that over the years, the word *"justice"* has come to mean something other than *"righteous."* *Webster's Dictionary* gives the word *"justice"* two meanings: Conformity of conduct or practice to the principles of right. (This agrees with the meaning of the biblical word we just discussed.) But then it adds the following definition: Vindictive retribution; merited punishment.

Over the years, the first meaning, "to practice the principles of right," has been replaced with the second meaning, "vindictive retribution or merited punishment."

In American society, if one has committed a wrong, then in order for justice to be done, it is believed that that person must receive punishment equal to the wrong they have committed. If that does not take place, then justice is not done. When one person violates another, until that person *"pays"* the penalty for what they have done, there is *no closure—no justice*.

Many people today are longing to see justice done in a situation where they have been wronged. But some of those people who claim to be Christians would not dare avenge themselves. They are counting on God to avenge the wrong another has done to them. To them, this is one of God's precious promises, *"vengeance is mine, I will repay, saith the Lord."* And they are anxious for the day the Lord gives their enemy what they so richly deserve!

The word *"vengeance"* in the verse quoted above is from the Greek word "ekdikesis" meaning, "a revenging, vengeance, punishment." Today, with the legal model of salvation, most people have come to understand God's justice in this same way. In order for God to be just, then He must impose an external arbitrary punishment upon those who have sinned in order that they pay for their wrong. Thus the expression "God is not only loving; He is just" arises.

That expression, as some others we have looked at, is not in the Bible, but this one is: *"For my thoughts are not your thoughts, neither are your ways my ways, saith the LORD. For as the heavens are higher than the earth, so are my ways higher than your ways, and my thoughts than your thoughts"* (Isaiah 55:8, 9).

Higher in what way? Maybe more noble, more righteous, more merciful, and more forgiving than we dare to think? In the Old Testament, God asked Job a meaningful question: *"Shall mortal man be more just than God?"* When God says, *"vengeance is mine; I will repay,"* does that mean God would do what we would do?

Let's look at that text in its context. Romans 12:17-21 says:

> "Recompense to no man evil for evil. Provide things honest in the sight of all men. If it be possible, as much as lieth in you, live peaceably with all men. Dearly beloved, avenge not yourselves, but rather give place unto wrath: for it is written, Vengeance is mine; I will repay, saith the Lord. Therefore if thine enemy hunger, feed him; if he thirst, give him drink: for in so doing thou shalt heap coals of fire on his head. Be not overcome of evil, but overcome evil with good."

What are these *"coals of fire?"* We find the answer in Song of Solomon 8:6: *"Set me as a seal upon thine heart, as a seal upon thine arm: for love is strong as death; jealousy is cruel as the grave: the coals thereof are coals of fire, which hath a most vehement flame."*

The *coals of fire* are love! In this context, it is clear that God expects us to overcome evil with good, with love. Would God not do the same? But words can be misleading. Many times we need examples. An experience in the life of the Apostle Paul gives us an illustration of how God's vengeance works.

"And they stoned Stephen, calling upon God, and saying, Lord Jesus, receive my spirit. And he kneeled down, and cried with a loud voice, Lord, lay not this sin to their charge. And when he had said this, he fell asleep. And Saul [Paul] was consenting unto his death. And at that time there was a great persecution against the church which was at Jerusalem....And devout men carried Stephen to his burial, and made great lamentation over him. As for Saul, he made havock of the church, entering into every house, and haling men and women committed them to prison" (Acts 7:59-8:3).

How will God bring Paul to justice? What will God do to see that Paul gets the punishment he so richly deserves?

"And Saul, yet breathing out threatenings and slaughter against the disciples of the Lord, went unto the high priest, And desired of him letters to Damascus to the synagogues, that if he found any of this way, whether they were men or women, he might bring them bound unto Jerusalem. And as he journeyed, he came near Damascus: and suddenly there shined round about him a light from heaven: And he fell to the earth, and heard a voice saying unto him, Saul, Saul, why persecutest thou me?

And he said, Who art thou, Lord?

And the Lord said, I am Jesus whom thou persecutest: it is hard for thee to kick against the pricks. And he trembling and astonished said, Lord, what wilt thou have me to do?" (Acts 9:1-6).

God converted Saul; he joined the disciples and was among the chief of the apostles! *"My ways are higher than your ways."* God's way is not to punish but to convert and reform. If we let God have His vengeance on our enemy, our enemy might be saved! Paul did suffer guilt for the things he had done, and he did suffer physically as well—beatings, stoning, imprisonment—but he did not suffer at God's hand.

Then there's the story of King Manasseh: *"Manasseh was twelve years old when he began to reign, and he reigned fifty and five years in Jerusalem: But did that which was evil in the sight of the LORD, like unto the abominations of the heathen, whom the LORD had cast out before the children of Israel. For he built again the high places which Hezekiah his father had broken down, and he reared up altars for Baalim, and made groves, and worshipped all the host of heaven, and served them"* (2 Chronicles 33:1-3).

How did God get even with Manasseh for what he had done? How did God make him pay?

> "So Manasseh made Judah and the inhabitants of Jerusalem to err, and to do worse than the heathen, whom the LORD had destroyed before the children of Israel. And the LORD spake to Manasseh, and to his people: but they would not hearken. Wherefore the LORD brought upon them the captains of the host of the king of Assyria, which took Manasseh among the thorns, and bound him with fetters, and carried him to Babylon. And when he was in affliction, he besought the LORD his God, and humbled himself greatly before the God of his fathers, And prayed unto him: and he was intreated of him, and heard his supplication, and brought him again to Jerusalem into his kingdom. Then Manasseh knew that the LORD he was God" (2 Chronicles 33:9-13).

God's way of taking vengeance on Manasseh was to help him see the error of his ways and bring him to the place of repentance.

Then there's the story of the nation of Israel God brought out of Egypt. With all their complaining and rebellion, what did God do to them? God graciously gave them what they needed. Where is the *justice* in that? In the end, He gave them His Son whom they rejected. What did God do to them then? On the Mount of Olives, He wept over them and then He left them. He didn't rain fire down from heaven upon them; He simply left them. And where are they today?

The term *"God is not only loving; He is just"* really implies a contradiction. It implies God is not only loving but He is vengeful. If you wrong Him, He will make you pay.

The term *"God is not only loving; He is just,"* is true only if understood in the true biblical meaning of the word *"just,"* which is *"right"* or *"righteous."* Then if we say, *"God is not only loving; He is righteous,"* we are saying God is loving, and He will always do the right thing, and the right thing is the loving thing. This is the true meaning of biblical justice, the true meaning of God's justice!

Can threatening talk about justice and vengeance and punishment serve any good purpose? The answer is yes, in certain situations, it can. You may remember a discussion we had in a previous chapter along these lines.

There are those in stages of immaturity, who, like children, sometimes need threatening language to help them avoid dangers in life. God is willing to meet people where they are and, even with the danger of being misunderstood, to use threatening language or action that will cause them to stop and listen. Then when He has their attention, He prefers to speak to them in the still small voice of His sweet Spirit.

The wonderful thing is that God loves us enough that He will do all He can, even risking His own reputation, to reach us so we will stop and listen! Therefore, let us be careful that we don't misunderstand the sometimes frightening or drastic methods God may use in emergency situations to be the way He is all the time.

God wants His children to grow up so He can speak to them as adults without threatening gestures or language. Yet, many still worship and obey God from fear, believing He will utterly destroy all His enemies. After all, He is Almighty God, and He has the ability and the right to do anything He wants to do. But, does that make it right for Him to do anything He wants? Can He be trusted with that kind of power?

That is one of the issues in the great controversy between Christ and Satan. But think about this: in the war between Christ and Satan, victory for God *is not* the destruction of His enemies. If it were, the war would last but a second. No, the victory for God *is to win* His enemies' love. God is not concerned with getting even (man's meaning of justice); God is concerned with doing what is right (God's meaning of justice). To love, to forgive, and to restore peace and harmony is right!

And if God's children reject Him and refuse His love, does that make it right for Him to burn them to death? God is love, and what is the only thing love can do to those who reject it? Beat them up; burn them up? No, the only thing real love can do to those who reject it is give them up! This will be discussed in more detail in the next chapter.

Chapter Ten

THE FINAL DEATH OF THE WICKED

"And I saw a great white throne, and him that sat on it, from whose face the earth and the heaven fled away; and there was found no place for them. And I saw the dead, small and great, stand before God; and the books were opened: and another book was opened, which is the book of life: and the dead were judged out of those things which were written in the books, according to their works. And the sea gave up the dead which were in it; and death and hell delivered up the dead which were in them: and they were judged every man according to their works. And death and hell were cast into the lake of fire. This is the second death. And whosoever was not found written in the book of life was cast into the lake of fire" (Revelation 20:11-15).

In this chapter, we will discuss how the wicked die. In previous chapters we have attempted to show that God is not the executioner of the wicked but that they die from the destructive effects of sin working within them as a deadly disease. The next question that comes to mind for many is, but what about the verse in Revelation that says *"and fire came down from God out of heaven and devoured them"*?

In the study of Revelation, we must be careful to identify symbolism. As we look at each new scene, we should ask, "Is this literal or symbolic?" Usually, if the statement or thing described makes no sense or violates the law of nature, we are to understand it as symbolic or figurative. With that in mind, note the following text:

"And when the thousand years are expired, Satan shall be loosed out of his prison, and shall go out to deceive the nations which are in the four quarters of

99

the earth, Gog and Magog, to gather them together to battle: the number of whom is as the sand of the sea. And they went up on the breadth of the earth, and compassed the camp of the saints about, and the beloved city: and fire came down from God out of heaven, and devoured them. And the devil that deceived them was cast into the lake of fire and brimstone, where the beast and the false prophet are, and shall be tormented day and night for ever and ever" (Revelation 20:7-10).

According to the rule of interpretation, is this to be taken literally or symbolically? We can understand much of it as literal. However, some things are obviously symbolic. Note, in one place it says the fire devours them, and then in the next sentence, it says the fire torments them forever and ever. The fire can't devour them and torment them forever at the same time! It makes no sense, so this part must be figurative.

Verses seven through ten constitute a summary statement. Then in verses eleven through fifteen, John describes another scene that gives us more detail concerning the event he just described in the previous verses.

After the Holy City comes down from heaven and the wicked are resurrected, Satan once again deceives them, and they come and "compass," or surround the city; thus setting the stage for the judgment.

"And I saw a great white throne, and him that sat on it, from whose face the earth and the heaven fled away; and there was found no place for them. And I saw the dead, small and great, stand before God; and the books were opened: and another book was opened, which is the book of life: and the dead were judged out of those things which were written in the books, according to their works. And the sea gave up the dead which were in it; and death and hell delivered up the dead which were in them" (Revelation 20:11-13).

This describes the *"second resurrection:"* the resurrection of the *"rest of the dead who lived not again until the thousand years were finished"* (Revelation 20:5) and the final phase of judgment.

Some have asked, "Why doesn't God just let them be? Why resurrect them again? Does He resurrect them only to judge and punish them, to see that they get what they deserve?" That would be reasonable in the legal model but not the healing model. Could it be that God intends to give them another chance to repent?

I believe God is doing as He has always done, He is demonstrating something of great significance to the entire universe. This is to be seen as another vital part of the answers in the great controversy regarding God's true nature and His government.

Isaiah prophesied that the time would come when *"all flesh,"* every human being, would see the glory of God at the same time. Isaiah 40:5 says, *"And the glory of the LORD shall be revealed, and all flesh shall see it together: for the mouth of the LORD hath spoken it."*

At the final judgment scene, all God's creatures, men and angels, who have been involved in the great controversy from the beginning to end, are gathered together at the same time and same place here on earth. All of the wicked are resurrected and stand outside the Holy City, while all the righteous are inside the Holy City. All are present at this climatic event at the close of the great controversy.

This is the time when *"the glory of the Lord shall be revealed."* What is His glory? You might remember that we discussed this question in a previous chapter. Moses asked the Lord to show him His glory. Exodus 33:18-23 records the story:

"And he [Moses] said, I beseech thee, shew me thy glory. And he [the Lord] said, I will make all my goodness pass before thee, and I will proclaim the name of the LORD before thee; and will be gracious to whom I will be gracious, and will shew mercy on whom I will shew mercy. And he said, Thou canst not see my face:

for there shall no man see me, and live. And the LORD said, Behold, there is a place by me, and thou shalt stand upon a rock: And it shall come to pass, while my glory passeth by, that I will put thee in a clift of the rock, and will cover thee with my hand while I pass by: And I will take away mine hand, and thou shalt see my back parts: but my face shall not be seen."

The account continues in Exodus 34:6, 7: *"And the LORD passed by before him, and proclaimed, The LORD, The LORD God, merciful and gracious, longsuffering, and abundant in goodness and truth, Keeping mercy for thousands, forgiving iniquity and transgression and sin."*

Note here that God's glory has two distinct facets: (1) The glory of His majesty and power that no mortal man can see and live—*"Our God is a consuming fire"* (Hebrews 12:29)—and (2) The _glory_ of His character of love and grace that Moses saw as the Lord passed by.

This is the _glory_ (character) of God that was also revealed in the person of Jesus Christ. The entire universe will see that together at the great white throne of judgment. *The Great Controversy* comments on the scene:

> "As soon as the books of record are opened, and the eye of Jesus looks upon the wicked, they are conscious of every sin which they have ever committed. They see just where their feet diverged from the path of purity and holiness, just how far pride and rebellion have carried them in the violation of the law of God. The seductive temptations which they encouraged by indulgence in sin, the blessings perverted, the messengers of God despised, the warnings rejected, the waves of mercy beaten back by the stubborn, unrepentant heart--all appear as if written in letters of fire. Above the throne is revealed the cross; and like a panoramic view appear the scenes of Adam's temptation and fall, and the successive steps in the great plan of redemption" (p. 666).

Romans 14:10 and 11 refers to this scene as well: *"For we shall all stand before the judgment seat of Christ. For it* is written, *As I live, saith the Lord, every knee shall bow to me, and every tongue shall confess to God."*

Note: *"we shall all stand before the judgment seat of Christ."* The difference is, some will be standing outside the city with the wicked, and some will be standing inside the city with Christ.

Philippians 2:10 and 11 refers to the same event: *"At the name of Jesus every knee should bow, of things in heaven, and things in earth, and things under the earth; And that every tongue should confess that Jesus Christ is Lord, to the glory of God the Father."*

"At the name of Jesus." Remember that in the Greek "name" is "onoma," which means not only one's title but their character as well. This means that as they see the glorious character of God in Christ so clearly displayed at the great white throne of judgment, everyone, even the wicked outside the walls, will acknowledge Him. But those outside the city walls, even though they acknowledge His glory, even though all their excuses to reject Christ have now been stripped away as they witness the love of God for them face-to-face, seeing it with their own eyes, they remain unrepentant as before.

The wicked at last come face-to-face with the enormity of their guilt as they see their wickedness in contrast to His righteousness, His glory. They are awakened to the result of their choices in life that have placed them outside *"the beloved city,"* and they are plunged into deep despair.

Luke 13:28 describes their anguish: *"There shall be weeping and gnashing of teeth, when ye shall see Abraham, and Isaac, and Jacob, and all the prophets, in the kingdom of God, and you yourselves thrust out."*

Now that they acknowledge the Lord's righteousness and bow before Him, would the Lord have mercy on them if they would now surrender their heart to Him? Before you answer, remember that God said, *"I change not."* He is the same *"yesterday, today, and forever."*

The Bible says, *"The mercy of the LORD is from everlasting to everlasting"* (Psalms 103:17). That means it never ends! So, instead of, "Will God give them another chance?", shouldn't the question be, "Since the wicked now see the truth about God so clearly, will they now surrender their hearts to Him?" Sadly, the answer is that even if God gave them another chance, they would not take advantage of it. They cannot find it in their hearts to repent.

Remember, to repent means to change. Just as Judas was sorry for betraying Jesus but could not find repentance, so the wicked find themselves in the same condition. At the great white throne of judgment, it will be clear that if even as the wicked witness everything God has done with their own eyes, they still *will not* repent.

In this way, the entire universe will witness the result of sin on the human heart. Sin changes people, not in a superficial or legal way, but sin, if not reversed or healed, changes and hardens the heart against God and His law of unselfish love to the point that there is no hope of recovery. They will never change. They can't; they are incurable. And being incurable, they will die.

God could prevent their death, but He has said that He *"will by no means clear the guilty."* He will give them up to *"reap that which they have sown."* But again, remembering God's ways are higher than ours, just how is He involved in the punishment of those for whom there is no hope?

The following is an important principle in understanding God's "punishment." According to the Bible, punishment is only administered in an attempt to bring forth the *"fruits of righteousness"* in a person. Note the following verse: *"Now no chastening for the present seemeth to be joyous, but grievous: nevertheless afterward it yieldeth the peaceable fruit of righteousness unto them which are exercised thereby"* (Hebrews 12:11).

God, as a loving father, *"chastens"* or trains, corrects, us to teach us the way of righteousness. But no good could possibly come from punishing the sinner after probation has closed and his heart is so hardened that it is clear there is no possibility for repentance or change. That is unless God wanted to send a message to the rest of the universe such as, *"In the future, you had better obey Me or this is what you'll get too!"*

But that would only result in obedience from fear, and God does not want that kind of obedience. The Bible says, *"perfect love casteth out fear: because fear hath torment"* (1 John 4:18). The punishment suffered by the wicked is the natural consequence of what they are and not some punishment God inflicts upon them.

Notice what the Bible says about the fire that destroys Satan: *"Thou hast defiled thy sanctuaries by the multitude of thine iniquities, by the iniquity of thy traffick; therefore will I bring forth a fire from the midst of thee, it shall devour thee, and I will bring thee to ashes upon the earth in the sight of all them that behold thee"* (Ezekiel 28:18).

What kind of fire *"comes forth from the midst"* of Satan? Note also the following texts about the cause of the destruction of the wicked.

- *"The righteous shall be in everlasting remembrance. He shall not be afraid of evil tidings: his heart is fixed, trusting in the LORD. His heart is established, he shall not be afraid, until he see his desire upon his enemies. He hath dispersed, he hath given to the poor; his righteousness endureth for ever; his horn shall be exalted with honour. The wicked shall see it, and be grieved; he shall gnash with his teeth, and melt away"* (Psalms 112:6-10).

- *"LORD, when thy hand is lifted up, they will not see: but they shall see, and be ashamed for their envy at the people; yea, the fire of thine enemies shall devour them"* (Isaiah 26:11).

- *"Ye shall conceive chaff, ye shall bring forth stubble: your breath* [Hebrew "ruwach"—spirit or character], *as fire, shall devour you. And the people shall be as the burnings of lime: as thorns cut up shall they be burned in the fire"* (Isaiah 33:11, 12).

All of these passages speak of a fire that comes from within, taking the life of the individual. It is the "fire" of severe emotional trauma. It is the fiery pain of despair, guilt, and self-condemnation that crushes out the life of the guilty on that fateful day. Since they have not confessed their guilt and let Christ bear it for them, they must bear it themselves, and it will crush them.

Ellen G. White writes, *"Calvary alone can reveal the terrible enormity of sin. If we had to bear our own guilt, it would crush us"* (*Thoughts from the Mount of Blessing*, p. 116).

Emotional pain and grief can cause great suffering and even death. According to a study published by Dr. Robert Kloner, a cardiologist at Good Samaritan Hospital in Los Angeles, he reports that during the January 17, 1994, Northridge/Los Angeles earthquake, over one hundred Californians literally died of fright. Apparently a terrorized brain can trigger the release of a mix of chemicals that causes the heart to contract and never relax again, thus leading to death (*Journal of the American College of Cardiology*, November 1, 1997, p. 1174-1180).

Medical scientists have discovered that extreme stress can cause the body to secrete excessive amounts of adrenalin, which can cause the heart to stop beating, resulting in death. This condition is known as the "broken heart syndrome." This is what I believe most of those outside the Holy City will experience on that day.

Again, they die as the result of what they have become, not something God is doing to them. It amazes me how men can believe that our gracious, compassionate, heavenly Father could burn His wayward children to death when we as mortal, sinful, selfish men could in no way bring ourselves do something as horrible as that to our children no matter how wicked we are. No, our God is not a King Nebuchadnezzar who has those who will not worship Him thrown into the fiery furnace to be burned to death!

But what about the *"fire that comes down from God out of heaven and devours them"*? The statement is clear, and we must deal with it. My response to the question is this: the wicked are already dead when the fire comes down and devours them. Let me give you the evidence for this conclusion.

First, the following text from Isaiah describes that same scene: *"And they shall go forth, and look upon the carcasses of the men that have transgressed against me: for their worm shall not die, neither shall their fire be quenched; and they shall be an abhorring unto all flesh"* (Isaiah 66:24). Note that it says, *"the carcasses of the men who have transgressed against me."* The fire is not burning people to death, but simply burning, or consuming the bodies of those who are already dead.

Next, Jesus spoke of the fire: *"And if thy hand offend thee, cut it off: it is better for thee to enter into life maimed, than having two hands to go into hell, into the fire that never shall be quenched"* (Mark 9:43).

The word "hell" is translated from the Greek word "gehenna," which refers to the valley of Gehinnon, a place south of Jerusalem that had become a trash dump. That was where the trash and the dead animals and the bodies of dead criminals, who had no relatives to bury them, were thrown out to be burned. They did not throw people alive into that fire; it was only dead bodies that were thrown into the fire.

Further evidence is found in Revelation 19:20 where it says the false prophet and the beast (systems, not individuals) were *"cast alive into a lake of fire,"* which implies that the fire will destroy and consume them. Then in Revelation 20:14, it says that the rest of the lost are simply "cast into the lake of fire." Since it does not make a point to say they are _alive_ when they are cast into the fire as it does in chapter nineteen, we can conclude they are already dead when they are cast into the fire.

Yet, more evidence is found in the Old Testament sacrificial system. David said in Psalms 73:3-5, _"For I was envious at the foolish, when I saw the prosperity of the wicked. For there are no bands in their death: but their strength is firm. They are not in trouble as other men; neither are they plagued like other men."_ Then verse seventeen says: _"Until I went into the sanctuary of God; then understood I their end."_

David said he didn't understand the fate of the wicked until he went to the sanctuary. The sacrifices made at the sanctuary pre-figured the death of the sinner as well as Christ's death since He died the death of the sinner. When the lamb was placed on the altar to be burned was it alive or dead? It was dead, of course. And, by the way, who killed the lamb? Not God, but the sinner. Who killed Christ, the Lamb of God? Sinners!

Note another sacrificial ceremony in Solomon's day referred to in 2 Chronicles 7:1: _"Now when Solomon had made an end of praying, the fire came down from heaven, and consumed the burnt offering and the sacrifices."_

In this passage, fire comes down from God out of heaven and devours the dead bodies of those animals on the altar, just as it will come down and consume the dead bodies of the wicked at the great white throne of judgment. I believe this is evidence enough to conclude that the wicked will be dead when _"fire comes down from God out of heaven and devours them."_

There is no question that there will be "fire" at God's presence in the end when God's glory is revealed. God's presence throughout the Bible is also described as fire.

- _"And the sight of the glory of the LORD was like devouring fire on the top of the mount in the eyes of the children of Israel"_ (Exodus 24:17).

- *"Thou shalt be visited of the LORD of hosts with thunder, and with earthquake, and great noise, with storm and tempest, and the flame of devouring fire"* (Isaiah 29:6).

- *"For our God is a consuming fire"* (Hebrews 12:29).

In Isaiah 33:14, a question is asked: *"Who among us shall dwell with the devouring fire? who among us shall dwell with everlasting burnings?"* The answer is given in verse fifteen and seventeen: *"He that walketh righteously, and speaketh uprightly....Thine eyes shall see the king in his beauty."*

The righteous will thrive in God's presence. But the wicked will die, and God will at last unveil His glory and the *"consuming fire"* will purify the earth of all its pollution as well as *"devour"* the dead bodies of the wicked. Peter speaks of this final consumption:

> "But the day of the Lord will come as a thief in the night; in the which the heavens shall pass away with a great noise, and the elements shall melt with fervent heat, the earth also and the works that are therein shall be burned up. Seeing then that all these things shall be dissolved, what manner of persons ought ye to be in all holy conversation and godliness, Looking for and hasting unto the coming of the day of God, wherein the heavens being on fire shall be dissolved, and the elements shall melt with fervent heat? Nevertheless we, according to his promise, look for new heavens and a new earth, wherein dwelleth righteousness" (2 Peter 3:10-13).

Now, the results of the great controversy between Christ and Satan are understood. The universe clearly sees that the wages of sin is death. Sin is the killer. God told the truth when He said, *"in the day you eat thereof you will surely die."* But they do not die the final second death at His gracious hand. Sin is the only source of death, and God did not create sin or death! They are alien intruders into His universe. God on the other hand is the only source of life! He is the only source of freedom, love, and every good and perfect gift.

Some people claim that teaching that God does not personally destroy the wicked portrays Him as *passive* or completely uninvolved or affected by the death of the wicked. That could not be farther from the truth. What will be your feelings as you look out at the wicked from the walls of the New Jerusalem on that day and watch the wicked die in mass turmoil, confusion, and agony when God finally unveils His glory and they are consumed by their guilt and despair? It may be that some of your loved ones are out there. Will you have feelings for them? Will you cry for them? Of course you will. If you are so hard hearted that the scene doesn't touch you, you won't be inside the New Jerusalem.

But then as we look into the face of our heavenly Father, will we see the face of a vengeful God who is gratified to see the wicked suffer, being satisfied that the penalty for His broken law is now being visited upon them? No, we will see the face of a loving, compassionate Father crying over His lost children as Jesus did over Jerusalem long ago. The wicked die a horrible death. The earth is consumed in fire. Sin and sinners are no more, and though God's heart is saddened, God's character of righteousness and love is vindicated. "God is not only loving; He is righteous! God is love!"

Now, at last there will be complete freedom in the universe, with everyone doing what is right because it is right, not because they are afraid not to, or because they have been fixed so they cannot sin. If God was going to fix us so we couldn't sin if we wanted to, we would be mere robots. And He could have done that in the beginning without going through this painful process.

I believe the most important question for the Christian to ask regarding the destruction of sin and sinners is, "How is God involved?" It is important because, as we discussed in a previous chapter, the picture we have of God makes a definite impression on our own character. If we picture God as arbitrary, vengeful, and severe, we will be too. If we believe God is the judge and executioner of the wicked, we may be in danger of taking part in, or at least supporting the end-time anti-Christ system that will persecute and execute those it judges as wicked sinners, *thinking they are doing God service* (John 16:2).

We should be very careful as to what we teach regarding God's character, lest we *"bear false witness of Him"* and distort the true gospel. But on the other hand, if we picture God as gracious, merciful, and righteous, like Jesus, we will be too. Remember, we will become like the God we worship.

In conclusion, we return to the symbolism of Revelation 20:14: *"And death and hell were cast into the lake of fire. This is the second death."*

How do you put death and the grave in the lake of fire? You can't. All of this is symbolic language too. Fire consumes, and at last the two enemies of God's people, death and the grave, will be consumed, destroyed forever. There will not be another resurrection, and there will be no more death. The righteous will reign with Christ in the earth made new forever!

You can be among those who will reign with Christ. The Bible says in 1 Peter 1:3, 4: *"Blessed be the God and Father of our Lord Jesus Christ, which according to his abundant mercy hath begotten us again unto a lively hope by the resurrection of Jesus Christ from the dead, To an inheritance incorruptible, and undefiled, and that fadeth not away, reserved in heaven for you."*

Reserved in heaven for YOU! The table is set and a place set aside just for you. The promise is real; Jesus took your place on the cross, but no one can take your place there. There will not only be an empty seat but an eternal void in God's heart if you are not there. If you have not already done so, begin now making your plans to be there!

Next, we will look at the subject that has troubled so many and many have questioned as to whether it could be possible. Perfection. Does God expect His people to be perfect? Jesus himself said, *"Be ye therefore perfect, even as your Father which is in heaven is perfect"* (Matthew 5:48). We will look at this question in the context of the healing model in the next chapter.

Chapter Eleven

SINLESS PERFECTION OR PERFECTLY HEALED?

"Be ye therefore perfect, even as your Father which is in heaven is perfect" (Matthew 5:48).

How many times have you heard someone say, "Nobody is perfect"? We all believe that to think of any human being as perfect is not realistic, but in Genesis 17:1, God said to Abram, *"I am the Almighty God; walk before me, and be thou perfect."* And in Deuteronomy 18:13, God said to Israel, *"Thou shalt be perfect with the Lord thy God."*

Again in Job 1:8, *"The LORD said unto Satan, Hast thou considered my servant Job, that there is none like him in the earth, a perfect and an upright man."* Then 1 Kings 15:14, speaking of Asa, one of King David's sons, it says, *"Asa's heart was perfect with the LORD all his days."*

As we search the New Testament, we find that the Apostle Paul says in 2 Corinthians 13:11: *"Finally, brethren....Be perfect, be of good comfort, be of one mind."* And then the words of Jesus in Matthew 5:48 plainly says, *"Be ye therefore perfect, even as your Father which is in heaven is perfect."*

If it is impossible for one to be perfect, then why has Jesus commanded it? And since Jesus has clearly given this command, shouldn't we take it seriously?

Maybe a good question to ask here would be, What did Jesus mean when He said for us to be perfect? Did He mean that we should come to the place where we live a perfect life, never committing sin, even in thought? Suppose you saw someone who never disobeyed their parents, never cursed, never gambled, never smoked or drank, never stole, never violated the Sabbath, never did anything wrong; would you be looking at a perfect person? You could be in a medical building looking at a well-preserved corpse. A corpse never does anything bad, but they never do anything good. They just never do anything!

This concept of perfection became rather popular in the early days of the church. Simeon Stylite, a member of the church in Antioch in the fourth century, became the number one proponent of this view. Stylite wanted to overcome sin so badly that he built a sixty-foot-tall pillar and climbed up on top. Stylite perched up on top of that pillar for 30 years until he died.

Now think of all the bad things you can't do up on top of a sixty-foot pillar. The other members of the church envied him with his perfect life and many of them built pillars for themselves, and pretty soon, all around the area there were church members perched up on pillars. Stylite founded a whole order in the church known as the "Stylites, the Order of the Pole Sitters."

This was the period when many would-be saints began to lock themselves away in monasteries. The idea was to place themselves where it was not possible to do anything wrong. Is this how the saints are going to be found when the Lord comes? Perched on pillars or locked in monasteries, no use to anybody, but never doing anything wrong.

Throughout history, many have sought the perfect environment where they would not be tempted to do wrong. Which brings up the question, would a perfect person, living in a perfect environment, insure that one would not sin? This was not enough for Lucifer or for Adam, both *"perfect,"* sinless beings in a *"perfect,"* sinless environment, yet both sinned. Obviously the absence of doing wrong cannot be the correct view of perfection. This is certainly not what Jesus meant when He said we were to be perfect.

The *Desire of Ages* helps us with the answer as to what Jesus was saying in this thoughtful statement: *"God's ideal for His children is higher than the highest human thought can reach. 'Be ye therefore perfect, even as your Father which is in heaven is perfect.' This command is a promise"* (p. 311).

"This command is a promise." I like that. If it is a promise, then it's not a demand, it's not something we do on our own, it's something God does in us! And that makes a big difference.

As we continue our search for truth, as always, we go to the original languages and find the definition of the word we are considering, in this case the word *"perfect."*

The Old Testament Hebrew word *"perfect"* is translated from *"tamin,"* which means *"whole"* or *"complete."* The New Testament Greek word is translated from *"telios,"* which carries the same meaning, *"whole"* or *"complete."*

Both words mean *"complete"* in the sense of being fully grown and mature or a work that has been completed. So when the Lord said, *"be ye therefore perfect,"* He is saying, *"you are to be grown-up, to be mature, to be complete."*

This process should begin at conversion, when one is won back to trust God. The change here is so great Jesus said it was like being *born again.* *"Except a man be born again, he cannot see the kingdom of God"* (John 3:3). In Romans 6:4, Paul writes that baptism best symbolizes this great change: *"Therefore we are buried with him by baptism into death: that like as Christ was raised up from the dead by the glory of the Father, even so we also should walk in newness of life."*

At this stage, the Christian is just a babe, and here is where the whole marvelous procedure of growing and healing begins. God loves His "babes," but He knows it is dangerous for them to stay in that stage of dependency. Babies need to grow up and care for themselves.

Note the following passages that deal with growing up or "perfection."

> "For when for the time ye ought to be teachers, ye have need that one teach you again which be the first principles of the oracles of God; and are become such as have need of milk, and not of strong meat. For every one that useth milk is unskilful in the word of righteousness: for he is a babe. But strong meat belongeth to them that are of full age, even those who by reason of use have their senses exercised to discern both good and evil.
>
> Therefore leaving the principles of the doctrine of Christ, let us go on unto perfection; not laying again the foundation of repentance from dead works, and of faith toward God" (Hebrews 5:12-6:1).

"Let us go on to perfection." In other words, let us go on to maturity, to grow up, to be no more babes but mature adults in the faith. Ephesians 4:11-15 provides additional insight:

> "And he gave some, apostles; and some, prophets; and some, evangelists; and some, pastors and teachers; For the perfecting of the saints, for the work of the ministry, for the edifying of the body of Christ: Till we all come in the unity of the faith, and of the knowledge of the Son of God, unto a perfect man, unto the measure of the stature of the fulness of Christ: That we henceforth be no more children, tossed to and fro, and carried about with every wind of doctrine, by the sleight of men, and cunning craftiness, whereby they lie in wait to deceive; But speaking the truth in love, may grow up into him in all things, which is the head, even Christ."

This is one purpose of the church, to help people grow up to perfection or maturity. It is not an arbitrary requirement that we grow up, but there are consequences if we remain babes. Chances are we will not survive the trials in life. The books of Daniel and Revelation tell us in the last days that we face a time of deception and confusion such as the world has never seen. As a church, we will not survive that final time of trouble if we are still babes in the truth.

So in mercy, God waits for His people to grow up and be settled into the truth. The latter rain, or the outpouring of the Holy Spirit, cannot come until God's children have matured to the point they can handle that kind of power. I believe this is the reason for the delay in Christ's coming; Christ is waiting on His bride to *"make herself ready."*

Another way to look at perfection, as we alluded to briefly before, is perfect obedience to God's law. A perfect person is perfectly obedient. That might sound legalistic until one takes a closer look at God's law. Let me explain.

Properly understood, as we discussed in chapter five, God's law does not take away our freedom. All God asks of us is to love as described in 1 Corinthians 13:4-8: *"Charity [love] suffereth long, and is kind; charity envieth not; charity vaunteth not itself, is not puffed up; doth not behave itself unseemly, seeketh not her own, is not easily provoked, thinketh no evil; rejoiceth not in iniquity, but rejoiceth in the truth; beareth all things, believeth all things, hopeth all things, endureth all things. Charity never faileth."*

To really obey God's commandments is simply to grow up in love: love for God and our fellowman. *"For all the law is fulfilled in one word, even in this; Thou shalt love thy neighbor as thyself"* (Galatians 5:14).

So how do we grow up like this? How do we become mature or complete? Ephesians 2:8 says, *"For by grace are ye saved* [remember the Greek word translated saved is "sozo," meaning "made whole" or, to mature, to grow up] *through faith."* We grow up *through faith;* that is through trusting in Christ. Remember the principle we discussed back in chapter two: *"By beholding we are changed into the same image."*

We either become like our idols—*"The idols of the heathen are silver and gold, the work of men's hands. They that make them are like unto them: so is every one that trusteth in them"* (Psalms 135:15, 18)—or we become like Jesus—*"But we all, with open face beholding as in a glass the glory of the Lord, are changed into the same image from glory to glory, even as by the Spirit of the Lord"* (2 Corinthians 3:18).

Again, it is important that we realize that being saved is not an event, it is a process, a process of maturing and healing that continues until we die or until Jesus returns. Let's read more of the comments from *The Desire of Ages*, from which we quoted earlier.

> "Be ye therefore perfect, even as your Father which is in heaven is perfect." This command is a promise. The plan of redemption contemplates our complete recovery from the power of Satan. Christ always separates the soul from sin .... He has made provision that the Holy Spirit shall be imparted to every repentant soul, to keep him from sinning. The tempter's agency is not to be accounted an excuse for one wrong act. Satan is jubilant when he hears the professed followers of Christ making excuses for their deformity of character. It is these excuses that lead to sin. There is no excuse for sinning. A holy temper, a Christlike life, is accessible to every repenting, believing child of God" (p. 311).

Do we want to stay *babes in Christ* for the rest of our lives, Being blown about by every wind of doctrine and needing someone to take care of us all the time? Or do we want to grow up and live that Christ-like life?

When we go to the doctor, do we want complete recovery? Or do we think, since *"nobody can be perfect,"* I just hope to get a little better? Note the words of Hebrews 7:25 about the extent to which salvation will be completed: *"Wherefore he is able also to save them to the uttermost that come unto God by him, seeing he ever liveth to make intercession for them."*

"He is able to save [to heal] *them to the uttermost."* Because of its preoccupation with being forgiven, the *le-*

gal model of salvation falls short of this ideal of being completely restored. How sad it is that God's promise of perfection, that is, complete recovery, perfect healing of our sin-sickness, is seen by many as impossible to obtain and is simply ignored.

Perfection has become a subject of much heated debate for some, but after examining the plan of salvation in light of the healing model, I believe we can see perfection, not as a legal requirement, but as a precious promise to those who realize they need God's healing. *"He which hath begun a good work in you will perform it"* (Philippians 1:6).

Perfection is not a command, and our part is not to heal ourselves, but as Jesus said to the paralytic at the pool, *"Would you like to be made whole?"* As the Great Physician, God has offered to make us completely whole, completely well, to completely heal all the damage done by the infection of sin. Our part is to cooperate with Him. People who are willing to do this are safe to save, no matter how much healing or growth may be needed.

And we have the assurance that even if our lives are cut short before the healing process is completed, as long as we are trusting in Him, we will be saved. When Jesus comes again He will complete the work He has begun in us! Then, we can live in a perfect place with perfect people and not be a danger to them because we have trusted and followed the directions of the Great Physician.

So we conclude with this truth from Jesus Himself: *"Be ye therefore perfect."* This is not a command but a personal and generous offer to each one of us that if we will fully surrender our hearts to Jesus, placing our trust in Him, we will "be perfect," that is, we will grow up and be completely healed. And one day, we will live among the saints and angels in the earth made new! How can we possibly turn down such an offer? I have accepted His offer and what a difference it has made in my life! I will share more about that in the next chapter.

Chapter Twelve

THE CONCLUSION OF THE MATTER

"When Jesus had lifted up himself, and saw none but the woman, he said unto her, Woman, where are those thine accusers? hath no man condemned thee? She said, No man, Lord. And Jesus said unto her, Neither do I condemn thee: go, and sin no more. Then spake Jesus again unto them, saying, I am the light of the world: he that followeth me shall not walk in darkness, but shall have the light of life"(John 8:10-12).

While I have attempted to provide the reader of this book with sufficient information to support the truth of the message it contains, it is not exhaustive. I have found that once a person grasps the basic revelation of this truth about the character of God and the healing model of salvation, that the Holy Spirit will lead them to confirmation and a deeper understanding as they continue to study God's Word.

My personal testimony, put in the context of the healing model, is this: I have been seeing the Great Physician for quite some time now, and while I am not completely healed, there has been great improvement in my overall health, both spiritually and physically, and I owe it all to Him!

As I look back on my life and the time I first accepted Christ, there have been many changes. It seems that God has revealed Himself more and more fully to my mind. Little by little over the years, as my rebellious attitude would allow Him, He has succeeded in bringing me to the place I am today. Not that I do not have a ways to go; I do. But I also realize that I have come a long way.

The most significant change in my heart, other than when I first accepted Christ, is when I began to see this picture of God and began to see how good He really is! I then realized it is true, by beholding Him we are changed.

Coming to see God in this new light and realizing that He does not condemn, but rather saves and heals, and that we have nothing whatsoever to fear from our heavenly Father, has made a tremendous difference in my character.

In the past, while claiming to be a Christian, teaching a church class, and even preaching from the pulpit, I used to look upon those whom I considered sinners as unworthy and condemned them in my heart, because I thought surely God felt the same way about them too. But now, I realize how wrong I was.

Now, I am able to see the sinner as God sees him, and now, I do not condemn or judge, but my heart longs to reach out to them, to help them find the Great Physician who did so much to help me! Since then, I have seen the healing-model picture of God have the same effect on others as well.

This understanding of God's gracious character can make the same difference in your life as it has in others. It can bring real peace and joy into your heart. It is the kind of thing that you can't keep silent about. You've got to share this good news! I believe this picture of God is the true gospel, the good news that God is not what His enemies have made Him out to be, but rather God is like Jesus! This picture of God is the everlasting gospel of Revelation 14 and a vital part of the message that the church must have and share before Jesus comes again.

1 John 3:2 says, *"Beloved, now are we the sons of God, and it doth not yet appear what we shall be: but we know that, when he shall appear, we shall be like him; for we shall see him as he is."*

We shall be like Him, and He is like God. If we are to be like Him, we must have the true picture of God, otherwise we will portray a false image of Him. I believe we find that true picture, not in a legal model, but in a model based on healing and trust: the healing model. We find this model in Jesus Christ as we trust in the Great Physician to restore us into the image of God, the image that He intended for us to have from the beginning.

My prayer is that if this is the first time you have seen this view, that your eyes have been opened more fully to the beauty of Him who is altogether lovely, that you will become more and more like Him as you continue to behold Him day by day. Or, if you already hold this picture of God in your heart, I hope that you will be more fully convinced of its truth.

Prophets and Kings (p. 314–315) sums up the message of this book so well:

> "In the vision that came to Isaiah in the temple court, he was given a clear view of the character of the God of Israel. 'The high and lofty One that inhabiteth eternity, whose name is Holy,' had appeared before him in great majesty; yet the prophet was made to understand the compassionate nature of his Lord. He who dwells 'in the high and holy place' dwells 'with him also that is of a contrite and humble spirit, to revive the spirit of the humble, and to revive the heart of the contrite ones.' Isaiah 57:15. The angel commissioned to touch Isaiah's lips had brought to him the message, 'Thine iniquity is taken away, and thy sin purged.' Isaiah 6:7.
>
> In beholding his God, the prophet, like Saul of Tarsus at the gate of Damascus, had not only been given a view of his own unworthiness; there had come to his humbled heart the assurance of forgiveness, full and free; and he had arisen a changed man. He had seen his Lord. He had caught a glimpse of the loveliness of the divine character. He could testify of the transformation wrought through beholding Infinite Love. Henceforth he was inspired with longing desire to see erring Israel set free from the burden and penalty of sin. 'Why

should ye be stricken any more?' the prophet inquired. 'Come now, and let us reason together, saith the Lord: though your sins be as scarlet, they shall be as white as snow; though they be red like crimson, they shall be as wool.' 'Wash you, make you clean; put away the evil of your doings from before Mine eyes; cease to do evil; learn to do well.' Isaiah 1:5, 18, 16, 17.

The God whom they had been claiming to serve, but whose character they had misunderstood, was set before them as the great Healer of spiritual disease. What though the whole head was sick and the whole heart faint? what though from the sole of the foot even unto the crown of the head there was no soundness, but wounds, and bruises, and putrefying sores? See Isaiah 1:6. He who had been walking frowardly in the way of his heart might find healing by turning to the Lord. 'I have seen his ways,' the Lord declared, 'and will heal him: I will lead him also, and restore comforts unto him....Peace, peace to him that is far off, and to him that is near, saith the Lord; and I will heal him.'" Isaiah 57:18, 19.

We'd love to have you download our
catalog of titles we publish at:

www.TEACHServices.com

or write or email us your thoughts,
reactions, or criticism about this
or any other book we publish at:

TEACH Services, Inc.
254 Donovan Road
Brushton, New York 12916

info@TEACHServices.com

or you may call us at:
518/358-3494

www.ingramcontent.com/pod-product-compliance
Lightning Source LLC
Chambersburg PA
CBHW060541100426
42742CB00013B/2408